The
APPLAUSE
of
HEAVEN

The
APPLAUSE
of
HEAVEN

MAX LUCADO

THOMAS NELSON
Since 1798

NASHVILLE DALLAS MEXICO CITY RIO DE JANEIRO

Published in Nashville, Tennessee, by Thomas Nelson. Thomas Nelson is a registered trademark of Thomas Nelson, Inc.

Thomas Nelson, Inc., titles may be purchased in bulk for educational, business, fund-raising, or sales promotional use. For information, please e-mail SpecialMarkets@ThomasNelson.com.

Unless otherwise noted, scripture quotations are from the Holy Bible, New International Version®, NIV®. Copyright © 1973, 1978, 1984 by Biblica, Inc.™ Used by permission of Zondervan. All rights reserved worldwide. *www.zondervan.com*

Scripture quotations marked TLB are from *The Living Bible*. © 1971. Used by permission of Tyndale House Publishers, Inc., Wheaton, Illinois 60189. All rights reserved.

Scripture quotations marked NEB are from THE NEW ENGLISH BIBLE. © 1961, 1970 by The Delegates of the Oxford University Press and the Syndics of the Cambridge University Press. Reprinted by permission.

Scripture quotations marked PHILLIPS are from J. B. Phillips: THE NEW TESTAMENT IN MODERN ENGLISH, Revised Edition. © J. B. Phillips 1958, 1960, 1972. Used by permission of Macmillan Publishing Co., Inc.

ISBN 978-0-8499-4632-5 (SE)
ISBN 978-0-8499-2123-0 (BSE)
ISBN 978-0-8499-4750-6 (Trade paper Repack)

The Library of Congress has cataloged the earlier edition as follows:

Lucado, Max.
The applause of heaven / Max Lucado.
p. cm.
ISBN 978-0-8499-1324-2 (HC)
1. Beatitudes=Devotional literature. I. Title.
bt382.l8 1990
226.9´306=dc20 90–39315

Printed in the United States of America

13 14 15 16 17 RRD 6 5 4 3 2 1

To Stanley Shipp, my father in the faith

CONTENTS

Contents

CONTENTS

FOREWORD

GOD SAYS ALL THE BIG WORDS IN OUR LIVES. STILL, IT IS OFT-times the little words that make the Big Word sing. Max Lucado is a rare and welcome talent who is dedicated to the Word made flesh, but is also a spellbinding spinner of such smaller words as may ornament God's Word.

I first discovered Lucado when I casually took *No Wonder They Call Him the Savior* off a bookstore shelf. Nothing was casual after his first line hooked my eye. Lucado has become popular for two reasons: he reveres Christ, and he loves the world around him. This double love binds our minds and beckons us to follow closely to see where his paragraphs may lead.

It is because Max Lucado loves his Lord that he turns from the muddlesome and thumbworn language so common in the church. To Lucado, Jesus is no ordinary noun to be theologized into dullness. Rather, all holy relationships are glorious, and only the best, most creative English is worthy. So he weaves anew the Shroud of Turin, leaving us no doubt that this splendid cloth has touched the body of our Lord and has been forever marked by the imprimatur of Lucado's reverence. Where no ordinary words will serve, here's how he bids us know the Christ:

"Sacred delight derives from stubborn joy," he exults.

"If you have time to read this chapter, you probably don't need to," he calls to those who think they're too busy for the spiritual disciplines.

On and on his wisdom flows: "Show a man his failures without Jesus, and the result will be found in the roadside gutter. Give a man religion without reminding him of his filth, and the result will be arrogance in a three-piece suit."

He counsels the arrogant that facing Christ is like entering the Church of the Nativity: "The door is so low, you can't go in standing up."

He rebukes the bitter: "Hatred is the rabid dog that turns on its owner. . . . The very word grudge starts with . . . GRRR . . . a growl!"

This book introduces the Beatitudes, which introduce the Sermon on the Mount. The Beatitudes fly at us, but in the simple metaphors of ordinary life. So you'll meet Christ even as you meet the *Exxon Valdez* that dark March night in 1989, when she spilled her crude venom on Bligh Reef in Alaska. The Christ of communion will come to you as you meet Gayaney Petroysan, an Armenian four years old who begged her mother's blood to live. And any number of great Bible heroes come and go in this book to make real the introduction to Jesus' great Sermon on the Mount.

Max and I are friends. I may have overpressed him to be my friend, and I will admit the friendship was originally my idea. But, I confess, I wanted to know Christ as Max does. I wanted to feel the April wind that breathed upon the cross, as he does. I wanted to fall like Thomas before Christ and cry, "My Lord and my God!" as he does. I needed Max to give me lessons on obedience and spiritual need.

Read this book in a quiet place and you may feel a wounded hand fall lightly on your shoulder. Be not afraid of the nearness you will feel to Christ, but go on and walk his paragraphs. Then you will know by experience that Lucado travels the high country of the Galilee of the heart.

CALVIN MILLER

BEFORE YOU BEGIN

THIS BOOK WAS ALMOST AS DIFFICULT TO TITLE AS IT WAS TO write. We went through list after list of options. Dozens of titles were suggested and dozens were discarded. Carol Bartley, Dave Moberg, the late Kip Jordon, and others at Word Publishing spent hours searching for the appropriate phrase that would describe the heart of the book.

In my mind, the scales were tipped in favor of *The Applause of Heaven* when my editor, Carol, read part of the manuscript to some of the Word executives. She read a portion of the book that describes our final journey into the city of God. She read some thoughts I wrote about God's hunger to have his children home, about how he longs to welcome us and may even applaud when we enter the gates.

After Carol read this section, she noticed one of the men was brushing away a tear. He explained his emotion by saying, "It's hard for me to imagine God applauding for me."

Can you relate?

I can. Certain things about God are easy to imagine. I can imagine him creating the world and suspending the stars. I can envision him as almighty, all-powerful, and in control. I can fathom a God who knows me, who made me, and I can even fathom a God who hears me. But a God who is in love with me? A God who is crazy for me? A God who cheers for me?

But that is the message of the Bible. Our Father is relentlessly in pursuit of his children. He has called us home with his Word, paved the path with his blood, and is longing for our arrival.

God's love for his children is the message of the Bible. And that is the message of this book.

Indulge me as I say thank-you to some dear friends who made this project possible.

First, to Calvin Miller. In 1977, a dear friend gave me a rectangular-shaped book called *The Singer* and urged me to read it. I did . . . several times. I was amazed. Never had I seen such word crafting. Never had I seen such passion. I still have the book on my shelf. It is dog-eared, weatherworn, and coffee stained.

But I will never discard it. For through it, Calvin Miller introduced me to a new caliber of writing—a fruitful hybrid of faith and creativity.

Thank you, Calvin, for what you've meant to thousands of readers over the last two decades. Thank you for sitting patiently until God gave you a fresh way to tell the ancient tale. And thank you for ushering this writer into a new palace of possibilities.

Thanks, also:

To Kip Jordon and Byron Williamson, two dear brothers who helped Word Publishing to be a ministry as well as a business.

To Ernie Owen, a Christian sage with one eye on him and the other on his children. Thanks for the counsel.

To Carol Bartley and Anne Christian Buchanan. Thanks for editing and editing and editing and editing and . . . You did a great job. (All my mistakes are our little secret, OK?)

To Mary Stain. Because of your secretarial skills and remarkable flexibility, another manuscript is completed. I'm grateful.

To the rest of the Oak Hills Church staff. What would I do without friends like you? Thank you so much.

To Tim Kimmel and John Trent. One conversation with you guys gives me enough encouragement for a whole month.

To the Oak Hills elders and church. I never dreamed I would have the privilege of serving with such a faithful family. I thank God for what he is doing.

To Dave Moberg, Nancy Guthrie, and David Edmonson, for making me look better than I really do.

To Michael Card, a troubadour of truth whose heart touches mine.

And lastly, two special people.

To my wife, Denalyn. Thank you for making coming home the highlight of my day.

And thanks to you, the reader, for spending your time and money in hopes of seeing Jesus. May he honor the desire of your heart.

NOW WHEN HE SAW THE CROWDS, HE WENT UP ON A MOUNTAIN-side and sat down. His disciples came to him, and he began to teach them, saying:

> *Blessed are the poor in spirit,*
>> *for theirs is the kingdom of heaven.*
> *Blessed are those who mourn,*
>> *for they will be comforted.*
> *Blessed are the meek,*
>> *for they will inherit the earth.*
> *Blessed are those who hunger and thirst for righteousness,*
>> *for they will be filled.*
> *Blessed are the merciful,*
>> *for they will be shown mercy.*
> *Blessed are the pure in heart,*
>> *for they will see God.*
> *Blessed are the peacemakers,*
>> *for they will be called sons of God.*
> *Blessed are those who are persecuted because of righteousness,*
>> *for theirs is the kingdom of heaven.*

MATTHEW 5:1–10

CHAPTER ONE

SACRED DELIGHT

Blessed . . .

SHE HAS EVERY REASON TO BE BITTER.

Though talented, she went unrecognized for years. Prestigious opera circles closed their ranks when she tried to enter. American critics ignored her compelling voice. She was repeatedly rejected for parts for which she easily qualified. It was only after she went to Europe and won the hearts of tough-to-please European audiences that stateside opinion leaders acknowledged her talent.

Not only has her professional life been a battle, her personal life has been marked by challenge. She is the mother of two handicapped children, one of whom is severely retarded. Years ago, in order to escape the pace of New York City, she purchased a home on Martha's Vineyard.

It burned to the ground two days before she was to move in.

Professional rejection. Personal setbacks. Perfect soil for the seeds of bitterness. A receptive field for the roots of resentment. But in this case, anger found no home.

Her friends don't call her bitter; they call her "Bubbles."

Beverly Sills. Internationally acclaimed opera singer. Retired director of the New York City Opera.

Her phrases are sugared with laughter. Her face is softened with serenity. Upon interviewing her, Mike Wallace stated that "she is one of the most impressive—if not *the* most impressive—ladies I've ever interviewed."

How can a person handle such professional rejection and personal trauma and still be known as Bubbles? "I choose to be cheerful," she says. "Years ago I knew I had little or no choice about success, circumstances, or even happiness; but I knew I could choose to be cheerful."

⟡

"We have prayed for healing. God has not given it. But he has blessed us."

Glyn spoke slowly. Partly because of her conviction. Partly because of her disease. Her husband, Don, sat in the chair next to her. The three of us had come together to plan a funeral—hers. And now, with that task done, with the hymns selected and the directions given, Glyn spoke.

"He has given us strength we did not know.

"He gave it when we needed it and not before." Her words were slurred, but clear. Her eyes were moist, but confident.

I wondered what it would be like to have my life taken from me at age forty-five. I wondered what it would be like to say good-bye to my children and spouse. I wondered what it would be like to be a witness to my own death.

"God has given us peace in our pain. He covers us all the time. Even when we are out of control, he is still there."

It had been a year since Glyn and Don had learned of Glyn's condition—amyotrophic lateral sclerosis (Lou Gehrig's disease). The cause and the cure remain a mystery. But the result doesn't. Muscle strength and mobility steadily deteriorate, leaving only the mind and the faith.

And it was the coming together of Glyn's mind and faith that caused me to realize I was doing more than planning a funeral. I was beholding holy jewels she had quarried out of the mine of despair.

"We can use any tragedy as a stumbling block or a stepping stone. . . .

"I hope this will not cause my family to be bitter. I hope I can be an example that God is wanting us to trust in the good times and the bad. For if we don't trust when times are tough, we don't trust at all."

Don held her hand. He wiped her tears. He wiped his own.

"Who are these two?" I asked myself as I watched him touch a tissue to her cheek. "Who are these, who, on the edge of life's river, can look across with such faith?"

The moment was solemn and sweet. I said little. One is not bold in the presence of the sacred.

"I have everything I need for joy!" Robert Reed said.

"Amazing!" I thought.

His hands are twisted and his feet are useless. He can't bathe himself. He can't feed himself. He can't brush his teeth, comb his hair, or put on his underwear. His shirts are held together by strips of Velcro. His speech drags like a worn-out audio cassette.

Robert has cerebral palsy.

The disease keeps him from driving a car, riding a bike, and going for a walk. But it didn't keep him from graduating from high school or attending Abilene Christian University, from which he graduated with a degree in Latin. Having cerebral palsy didn't keep him from teaching at a St. Louis junior college or from venturing overseas on five mission trips.

And Robert's disease didn't prevent him from becoming a missionary in Portugal.

He moved to Lisbon, alone, in 1972. There he rented a hotel room and began studying Portuguese. He found a restaurant owner who would feed him after the rush hour and a tutor who would instruct him in the language.

Then he stationed himself daily in a park, where he distributed brochures about Christ. Within six years he led seventy people to the Lord, one of whom became his wife, Rosa.

I heard Robert speak recently. I watched other men carry him in his wheelchair onto the platform. I watched them lay a Bible in his lap. I watched his stiff fingers force open the pages. And I watched people in the audience wipe away tears of admiration from their faces. Robert could have asked for sympathy or pity, but he did just the opposite. He held his bent hand up in the air and boasted, "I have everything I need for joy."

His shirts are held together by Velcro, but his life is held together by joy.

No man had more reason to be miserable than this one—yet no man was more joyful.

His first home was a palace. Servants were at his fingertips. The snap of his fingers changed the course of history. His name was known and loved. He had everything—wealth, power, respect.

And then he had nothing.

Students of the event still ponder it. Historians stumble as they attempt to explain it. How could a king lose everything in one instant?

One moment he was royalty; the next he was in poverty.

His bed became, at best, a borrowed pallet—and usually the hard earth. He never owned even the most basic mode of transportation and was dependent upon handouts for his income. He was sometimes so hungry he would eat raw grain or pick fruit off a tree. He knew what it was like to be rained on, to be cold. He knew what it meant to have no home.

His palace grounds had been spotless; now he was exposed to filth. He had never known disease, but was now surrounded by illness.

In his kingdom he had been revered; now he was ridiculed. His neighbors tried to lynch him. Some called him a lunatic. His family tried to confine him to their house.

Those who didn't ridicule him tried to use him. They wanted favors. They wanted tricks. He was a novelty. They wanted to be seen with him—that is, until being with him was out of fashion. Then they wanted to kill him.

He was accused of a crime he never committed. Witnesses were hired to lie. The jury was rigged. No lawyer was assigned to his defense. A judge swayed by politics handed down the death penalty.

They killed him.

He left as he came—penniless. He was buried in a borrowed grave, his funeral financed by compassionate friends. Though he once had everything, he died with nothing.

He should have been miserable. He should have been bitter. He had every right to be a pot of boiling anger. But he wasn't.

He was joyful.

Sourpusses don't attract a following. People followed him wherever he went.

Children avoid soreheads. Children scampered after this man.

Crowds don't gather to listen to the woeful. Crowds clamored to hear him.

Why? He was joyful. He was joyful when he was poor. He was joyful when he was abandoned. He was joyful when he was betrayed. He was even joyful as he hung on a tool of torture, his hands pierced with six-inch Roman spikes.

Jesus embodied a stubborn joy. A joy that refused to bend in the wind of hard times. A joy that held its ground against pain. A joy whose roots extended deep into the bedrock of eternity.

Perhaps that's where Beverly Sills learned it. Without doubt, that is where Glyn Johnson and Robert Reed learned it. And that is where we can learn it.

What type of joy is this? What is this cheerfulness that dares to wink at adversity? What is this bird that sings while it is still dark? What is the source of this peace that defies pain?

I call it sacred delight.

It is sacred because it is not of the earth. What is sacred is God's. And this joy is God's.

It is delight because delight can both satisfy and surprise.

Delight is the Bethlehem shepherds dancing a jig outside a cave. Delight is Mary watching God sleep in a feed trough. Delight is white-haired Simeon praising God, who is about to be circumcised. Delight is Joseph teaching the Creator of the world how to hold a hammer.

Delight is the look on Andrew's face at the lunch pail that never came up empty. Delight is the dozing wedding guests who drank the wine that had been water. Delight is Jesus walking through waves as casually as you walk through curtains. Delight is a leper seeing a finger where there had been only a nub . . . a widow hosting a party with food made for a funeral . . . a paraplegic doing somersaults. Delight is Jesus doing impossible things in crazy ways: healing the blind with spit, paying taxes with a coin found in a fish's mouth, and coming back from the dead disguised as a gardener.

What is sacred delight? It is God doing what gods would be doing only in your wildest dreams—wearing diapers, riding donkeys, washing feet, dozing in storms. Delight is the day they accused God of having too much fun, attending too many parties, and spending too much time with the Happy Hour crowd.

Delight is the day's wage paid to workers who had worked only one hour . . . the father scrubbing the pig smell off his son's back . . . the shepherd throwing a party because the sheep was found. Delight is a discovered pearl, a multiplied talent, a heaven-bound beggar, a criminal in the kingdom. Delight is the surprise on the faces of street folks who have been invited to a king's banquet.

Delight is the Samaritan woman big-eyed and speechless, the adulteress walking out of the stone-cluttered courtyard, and a skivvy-clad Peter plunging into cold waters to get close to the one he'd cursed.

Sacred delight is good news coming through the back door of your heart. It's what you'd always dreamed but never expected. It's the too-good-to-be-true coming true. It's having God as your pinch-hitter, your lawyer, your dad, your biggest fan, and your best friend. God on your side, in your heart, out in front, and protecting your back. It's hope where you least expected it: a flower in life's sidewalk.

It is *sacred* because only God can grant it. It is a *delight* because it thrills. Since it is sacred, it can't be stolen. And since it is delightful, it can't be predicted.

It was this gladness that danced through the Red Sea. It was this joy that blew the trumpet at Jericho. It was this secret that made Mary sing. It was this surprise that put the springtime into Easter morning.

It is God's gladness. It's sacred delight.

And it is this sacred delight that Jesus promises in the Sermon on the Mount.

Nine times he promises it. And he promises it to an unlikely crowd:

- *"The poor in spirit."* Beggars in God's soup kitchen.
- *"Those who mourn."* Sinners Anonymous bound together by the truth of their introduction: "Hi, I am me. I'm a sinner."

- *"The meek."* Pawnshop pianos played by Van Cliburn. (He's so good no one notices the missing keys.)
- *"Those who hunger and thirst."* Famished orphans who know the difference between a TV dinner and a Thanksgiving feast.
- *"The merciful."* Winners of the million-dollar lottery who share the prize with their enemies.
- *"The pure in heart."* Physicians who love lepers and escape infection.
- *"The peacemakers."* Architects who build bridges with wood from a Roman cross.
- *"The persecuted."* Those who manage to keep an eye on heaven while walking through hell on earth.

It is to this band of pilgrims that God promises a special blessing. A heavenly joy. A sacred delight.

But this joy is not cheap. What Jesus promises is not a gimmick to give you goose bumps nor a mental attitude that has to be pumped up at pep rallies. No, Matthew 5 describes God's radical reconstruction of the heart.

Observe the sequence. First, we recognize we are in need (we're poor in spirit). Next, we repent of our self-sufficiency (we mourn). We quit calling the shots and surrender control to God (we're meek). So grateful are we for his presence that we yearn for more of him (we hunger and thirst). As we grow closer to him, we become more like him. We forgive others (we're merciful). We change our outlook (we're pure in heart). We love others (we're peacemakers). We endure injustice (we're persecuted).

It's no casual shift of attitude. It is a demolition of the old structure and a creation of the new. The more radical the change, the greater the joy. And it's worth every effort, for this is the joy of God.

It's no accident that the same word used by Jesus to promise sacred delight is the word used by Paul to describe God:

"The blessed God ..."[1]

"God, the blessed and only Ruler ... "[2]

Think about God's joy. What can cloud it? What can quench it? What can kill it? Is God ever in a bad mood because of bad weather? Does God get ruffled over long lines or traffic jams? Does God ever refuse to rotate the earth because his feelings are hurt?

No. His is a joy which consequences cannot quench. His is a peace which circumstances cannot steal.

There is a delicious gladness that comes from God. A holy joy. A sacred delight.

And it is within your reach. You are one decision away from Joy.

CHAPTER TWO

HIS SUMMIT

---

*Now when he saw the crowds, he went up
on a mountainside and sat down.*

If you have time to read this chapter, you probably don't need to.

If you are reading slowly in order to have something to occupy your time . . . if your reading hour is leisurely sandwiched between a long stroll and a good nap . . . if your list of things to do today was done an hour after you got up . . . then you might want to skip over to the next chapter. You probably have mastered the message of the next few pages.

If, however, you are reading in your car with one eye on the stoplight . . . or in the airport with one ear listening for your

---

flight . . . or in the baby's room with one hand rocking the crib . . . or in bed late at night, knowing you have to get up early in the morning . . . then read on, friend. This chapter is for you.

You are in a hurry. America is in a hurry. Time has skyrocketed in value. The value of any commodity depends on its scarcity. And time that once was abundant now is going to the highest bidder.

A man in Florida bills his ophthalmologist ninety dollars for keeping him waiting one hour.

A woman in California hires someone to do her shopping for her—out of a catalog.

Twenty bucks will pay someone to pick up your cleaning.

Fifteen hundred bucks will buy a fax machine . . . for your car.

Greeting cards can be purchased to express to your children things you want to say, but don't have time to: "Have a great day at school" or "I wish I were there to tuck you in."

America—the country of shortcuts and fast lanes. (We're the only nation on earth with a mountain called "Rushmore.")

"Time," according to pollster Louis Harris, "may have become the most precious commodity in the land."

Do we really have less time? Or is it just our imagination?

In 1965 a testimony before a Senate subcommittee claimed the future looked bright for free time in America. By 1985, predicted the report, Americans would be working twenty-two hours a week and would be able to retire at age thirty-eight.

The reason? The computer age would usher in a gleaming array of advances that would do our work for us while stabilizing our economy.

Take the household, they cited. Microwaves, quickfix foods, and food processors will pave the way into the carefree future.

And the office? Well, you know that old stencil machine? It'll be replaced by a copier. And the files? Computers are the files of the future. And that electric typewriter? Don't get too attached to it; a computer will do its work too.

And now, years later, we have everything the report promised. The computers are byting, the VCRs are recording, the fax machines are faxing. Yet the clocks are still ticking, and people are still running. The truth is, the average amount of leisure time has *shrunk* 37 percent since 1973. The average work week has *increased* from forty-one to forty-seven hours. (And, for many of you, forty-seven hours would be a calm week.)[1]

Why didn't the forecast come true? What did the committee overlook? They misjudged the appetite of the consumer. As the individualism of the sixties led to the materialism of the eighties, the free time gained for us by technology didn't make us relax; it made us run. Gadgets provided more time . . . more time meant more potential money . . . more potential money meant more time needed . . . and round and round it went. Lives grew louder as demands became greater. And as demands became greater, lives grew emptier.

"I've got so many irons in the fire, I can't keep any of them hot," complained one young father.

Can you relate?

When I was ten years old, my mother enrolled me in piano lessons. Now, many youngsters excel at the keyboard. Not me. Spending thirty minutes every afternoon tethered to a piano bench was a torture just one level away from swallowing broken glass. The metronome inspected each second with glacial slowness before it was allowed to pass.

Some of the music, though, I learned to enjoy. I hammered the staccatos. I belabored the crescendos.

The thundering finishes I kettle-drummed. But there was one instruction in the music I could never obey to my teacher's satisfaction. The rest. The zigzagged command to do nothing. Nothing! What sense does that make? Why sit at the piano and pause when you can pound?

"Because," my teacher patiently explained, "music is always sweeter after a rest."

It didn't make sense to me at age ten. But now, a few decades later, the words ring with wisdom—divine wisdom. In fact, the words of my teacher remind me of the convictions of another Teacher.

"When he saw the crowds, he went up on a mountain-side. . . ."

Don't read the sentence so fast you miss the surprise. Matthew didn't write what you would expect him to. The verse doesn't read, "When he saw the crowds, he went into their midst." Or "When he saw the crowds, he healed their hurts." Or "When he saw the crowds, he seated them and began to teach them." On other occasions he did that . . . but not this time.

Before he went to the masses, he went to the mountain. Before the disciples encountered the crowds, they encountered the Christ. And before they faced the people, they were reminded of the sacred.

I often write late at night. Not necessarily because I want to, but because sanity only comes to our house after the ten o'clock news.

From the moment I get home in the afternoon to the minute I sit down at this computer some five hours later, the motion is non-stop. Within thirty seconds of my entering the door, both of my knees are attacked by two squealing girls. A fuzzy-headed infant is placed in my arms and a welcome-home kiss is placed on my lips.

"The cavalry is here," I announce.

"And none too soon," my wife, Denalyn, replies with a grateful smile.

The next few hours bring a chorus of family noises: giggles, clanging dishes, rumbles on the floor, screams of agony over stumped toes, splashes in the bath, and thuds from toys tossed in the basket. The conversation is as continuous as it is predictable.

"Can I have more pie?"

"Jenna has my doll!"

"Can I hold the baby?"

"Honey, where is the pacifier?"

"Are there any clean gowns in the dryer?"

"Girls, it's time to go to bed."

"One more song?"

Then, eventually, the nightly hurricane passes, and the roar subsides. Mom looks at Dad. The day's damage is surveyed and cleaned up. Mom goes to bed, and Dad goes into the playroom to write.

That's where I am now. I sit in the stillness accompanied by the tap of a computer keyboard, the aroma of coffee, and the rhythm of the dishwasher. What was a playroom thirty minutes ago is now a study. And what is a study now may—just may—become a sanctuary. For what may happen in the next few minutes borders on the holy.

The quietness will slow my pulse, the silence will open my ears, and something sacred will happen. The soft slap of sandaled feet will break the stillness, a pierced hand will extend a quiet invitation, and I will follow.

I wish I could say it happens every night; it doesn't. Some nights he asks and I don't listen. Other nights he asks and I just don't go. But some nights I hear his poetic whisper, "Come to me, all you who are weary and burdened . . ."² and I follow. I leave behind the budgets, bills, and deadlines and walk the narrow trail up the mountain with him.

You've been there. You've escaped the sandy foundations of the valley and ascended his grand outcropping of granite. You've turned your back on the noise and sought his voice. You've stepped away from the masses and followed the Master as he led you up the winding path to the summit.

His summit. Clean air. Clear view. Crisp breeze. The roar of the marketplace is down there, and the perspective of the peak is up here.

Gently your guide invites you to sit on the rock above the tree line and look out with him at the ancient peaks that will never erode. "What is necessary is still what is sure," he confides. "Just remember:

"You'll go nowhere tomorrow that I haven't already been.

"Truth will still triumph.

"Death will still die.

"The victory is yours.

"And delight is one decision away—seize it."

The sacred summit. A place of permanence in a world of transition.

Think about the people in your world. Can't you tell the ones who have been to his mountain? Oh, their problems aren't any different. And their challenges are just as severe. But there is a stubborn peace that enshrines them. A confidence that life isn't toppled by unmet budgets or rerouted airplanes. A serenity that softens the corners of their lips. A contagious delight sparkling in their eyes.

And in their hearts reigns a fortresslike confidence that the valley can be endured, even enjoyed, because the mountain is only a decision away.

I read recently about a man who had breathed the summit air. His trips up the trail began early in his life and sustained him to the end. A few days before he died, a priest went to visit him in the hospital. As the priest entered the room, he noticed an empty chair beside the man's bed. The priest asked him if someone had been by to visit. The old man smiled, "I place Jesus on that chair, and I talk to him."

The priest was puzzled, so the man explained. "Years ago a friend told me that prayer was as simple as talking to a good friend. So every day I pull up a chair, invite Jesus to sit, and we have a good talk."

Some days later, the daughter of this man came to the parish house to inform the priest that her father had just died. "Because he seemed so content," she said, "I left him in his room alone for a couple of hours. When I got back to the room, I found him dead. I noticed a strange thing, though: his head was resting, not on the pillow, but on an empty chair that was beside his bed."[3]

Learn a lesson from the man with the chair. Make note of

the music teacher and the rest. Take a trip with the King to the mountain peak. It's pristine, uncrowded, and on top of the world. Stubborn joy begins by breathing deep up there before you go crazy down here.

Oops, I think I hear someone calling your flight. . . .

CHAPTER THREE

THE AFFLUENT POOR

Blessed are the poor in spirit . . .

WE COULD BEGIN WITH SARAI LAUGHING. HER WRINKLED FACE buried in bony hands. Her shoulders shaking. Her lungs wheezing. She knows she shouldn't laugh; it's not kosher to laugh at what God says. But just as she catches her breath and wipes away the tears, she thinks about it again—and a fresh wave of hilarity doubles her over.

We could begin with Peter staring. It's a stunned stare. His eyes are the size of grapefruits. He's oblivious to the fish piled to his knees and to the water lapping over the edge of the boat. He's deaf to the demands that he snap out of it and help. Peter is numb, absorbed in one thought—a thought too zany to say aloud.

We could begin with Paul resting. For three days he has wrestled; now he rests. He sits on the floor, in the corner. His face is haggard. His stomach is empty.

His lips are parched. Bags droop beneath the blinded eyes. But there is a slight smile on his lips. A fresh stream is flowing into a stagnant pool, and the water is sweet.

But let's not begin with these. Let's begin elsewhere.

Let's begin with the New Testament yuppie negotiating.

He's rich. Italian shoes. Tailored suit. His money is invested. His plastic is golden. He lives like he flies—first class.

He's young. He pumps away fatigue at the gym and slam-dunks old age on the court. His belly is flat, his eyes sharp. Energy is his trademark, and death is an eternity away.

He's powerful. If you don't think so, just ask him. You got questions? He's got answers. You got problems? He's got solutions. You got dilemmas? He's got opinions. He knows where he's going, and he'll be there tomorrow. He's the new generation. So the old had better pick up the pace or pack their bags.

He has mastered the three Ps of yuppiedom. Prosperity. Posterity. Power. He's the rich . . . young . . . ruler.[1]

Till today, life for him has been a smooth cruise down a neon avenue. But today he has a question. A casual concern or a genuine fear? We don't know. We do know he has come for some advice.

For one so used to calling the shots, calling on this carpenter's son for help must be awkward. For a man of his pedigree to seek the counsel of a country rube is not standard procedure. But this is no standard question.

"Teacher," he asks, "what good thing must I do to get eternal life?" The wording of his question betrays his misunderstanding. He thinks he can get eternal life as he gets everything else—by his own strength.

"What must *I* do?"

What are the requirements, Jesus? What's the break-even point? No need for chitchat; go straight to the bottom line. How much do I need to invest to be certain of my return?

Jesus' answer is intended to make him wince. "If you want to enter life, obey the commandments."

A man with half a conscience would have thrown up his hands at that point. "Keep the commandments? Keep the commandments! Do you know how many commandments there are? Have you read the Law lately? I've tried—honestly, I've tried—but I can't."

That is what the ruler should say, but confession is the farthest thing from his mind. Instead of asking for help, he grabs a pencil and paper and asks for the list.

"Which ones?" He licks his pencil and arches an eyebrow.

Jesus indulges him. "Do not murder, do not commit adultery, do not steal, do not give false testimony, honor your father and mother, and love your neighbor as yourself."

"Great!" thinks the yuppie as he finishes the notes. "Now I've got the quiz. Let's see if I pass.

"Murder? Of course not. Adultery? Well, nothing any red-blooded boy wouldn't do. Stealing? A little extortion, but all justifiable. False testimony? Hmmmm . . . let's move on. Honor your father and mother? Sure, I see them on holidays. Love your neighbor as yourself . . . ?

"Hey," he grins, "a piece of cake. I've done all of these. In fact, I've done them since I was a kid." He swaggers a bit and hooks a thumb in his belt. "Got any other commandments you want to run past me?"

How Jesus keeps from laughing—or crying—is beyond me. The question that was intended to show the ruler how he falls short only convinces him that he stands tall. He's a child dripping water on the floor while telling his mom he hasn't been in the rain.

Jesus gets to the point. "If you want to be perfect, then go sell your possessions and give to the poor, and you will have treasure in heaven."

The statement leaves the young man distraught and the disciples bewildered.

Their question could be ours: "Who then can be saved?"

Jesus' answer shell-shocks the listeners, "With man this is impossible. . . ."

Impossible.

He doesn't say improbable. He doesn't say unlikely. He doesn't even say it will be tough. He says it is "impossible." No chance. No way. No loopholes. No hope. Impossible. It's impossible to swim the Pacific. It's impossible to go to the moon on the tail of a kite. You can't climb Mount Everest with a picnic basket and a walking stick. And unless somebody does something, you don't have a chance of going to heaven.

Does that strike you as cold? All your life you've been rewarded according to your performance. You get grades according to your study. You get commendations according to your success. You get money in response to your work.

That's why the rich young ruler thought heaven was just a payment away. It only made sense. You work hard, you pay your dues, and "zap"—your account is credited as paid in full. Jesus says, "No way." What you want costs far more than what you can pay. You don't need a system, you need a Savior. You don't need a résumé, you need a Redeemer. For "what is impossible with men is possible with God."[2]

Don't miss the thrust of this verse: you *cannot save yourself.* Not through the right rituals. Not through the right doctrine. Not through the right devotion. Not through the right goose bumps. Jesus' point is crystal clear. It is impossible for human beings to save themselves.

You see, it wasn't the money that hindered the rich man; it was the self-sufficiency. It wasn't the possessions; it was the pomp. It wasn't the big bucks; it was the big head. "How hard it is for the rich to enter the kingdom of God!"[3] It's not just the rich who have difficulty. So do the educated, the strong, the good-looking, the popular, the religious. So do you if you think your piety or power qualifies you as a kingdom candidate.

And if you have trouble digesting what Jesus said to the rich young ruler, then his description of the judgment day will stick in your throat.

It's a prophetic picture of the final day: "Many will say to me on that day, 'Lord, Lord, did we not prophesy in your name, and in your name drive out demons and perform many miracles?'"[4]

Astounding. These people are standing before the throne of God and bragging about *themselves.* The great trumpet has sounded, and they are still tooting their own horns. Rather than sing his praises, they sing their own. Rather than worship God, they read their résumés. When they should be speechless, they speak. In the very aura of the King they boast of self. What is worse—their arrogance or their blindness?

You don't impress the officials at NASA with a paper airplane. You don't boast about your crayon sketches in the presence of Picasso. You don't claim equality with Einstein because you can write "H_2O."

And you don't boast about your goodness in the presence of the Perfect.

"Then I will tell them plainly, 'I never knew you. Away from me, you evildoers!'"[5]

Mark it down. God does not save us because of what we've done. Only a puny god could be bought with tithes. Only an egotistical god would be impressed with our pain. Only a temperamental god could be satisfied by sacrifices. Only a heartless god would sell salvation to the highest bidders.

And only a great God does for his children what they can't do for themselves.

That is the message of Paul: "For what the law was powerless to do . . . God did."[6]

And that is the message of the first beatitude.

"Blessed are the poor in spirit. . . ."

The jewel of joy is given to the impoverished spirits, not the affluent.[7] God's delight is received upon surrender, not awarded upon conquest. The first step to joy is a plea for help, an acknowledgment of moral destitution, an admission of inward paucity. Those who taste God's presence have declared spiritual bankruptcy and are aware of their spiritual crisis. Their cupboards are bare. Their pockets are empty. Their options are gone. They have long since stopped demanding justice; they are pleading for mercy.[8]

They don't brag; they beg.

They ask God to do for them what they can't do without him. They have seen how holy God is and how sinful they are and have agreed with Jesus' statement, "Salvation is impossible."

Oh, the irony of God's delight—born in the parched soil of destitution rather than the fertile ground of achievement.

It's a different path, a path we're not accustomed to taking. We don't often declare our impotence. Admission of failure is not usually admission into joy. Complete confession is not commonly followed by total pardon. But then again, God has never been governed by what is common.

CHAPTER FOUR

THE KINGDOM OF
THE ABSURD

. . . for theirs is the kingdom of heaven.

THE KINGDOM OF HEAVEN. ITS CITIZENS ARE DRUNK ON WONDER.

Consider the case of Sarai.[1] She is in her golden years, but God promises her a son. She gets excited. She visits the maternity shop and buys a few dresses. She plans her shower and remodels her tent . . . but no son. She eats a few birthday cakes and blows out a lot of candles . . . still no son. She goes through a decade of wall calendars . . . still no son.

So Sarai decides to take matters into her own hands. ("Maybe God needs me to take care of this one.")

She convinces Abram that time is running out. ("Face it, Abe, you ain't getting any younger, either.") She commands her maid, Hagar, to go into Abram's tent and see if he needs anything. ("And I mean 'anything'!") Hagar goes in a maid. She comes out a mom. And the problems begin.

Hagar is haughty. Sarai is jealous. Abram is dizzy from the dilemma. And God calls the baby boy a "wild donkey"—an appropriate name for one born out of stubbornness and destined to kick his way into history.

It isn't the cozy family Sarai expected. And it isn't a topic Abram and Sarai bring up very often at dinner.

Finally, fourteen years later, when Abram is pushing a century of years and Sarai ninety . . . when Abram has stopped listening to Sarai's advice, and Sarai has stopped giving it . . . when the wallpaper in the nursery is faded and the baby furniture is several seasons out of date . . . when the topic of the promised child brings sighs and tears and long looks into a silent sky . . . God pays them a visit and tells them they had better select a name for their new son.

Abram and Sarai have the same response: laughter. They laugh partly because it is too good to happen and partly because it might. They laugh because they have given up hope, and hope born anew is always funny before it is real.

They laugh at the lunacy of it all.

Abram looks over at Sarai—toothless and snoring in her rocker, head back and mouth wide open, as fruitful as a pitted prune and just as wrinkled. And he cracks up. He tries to contain it, but he can't. He has always been a sucker for a good joke.

Sarai is just as amused. When she hears the news, a cackle escapes before she can contain it. She mumbles something about her husband's needing a lot more than what he's got and then laughs again.

They laugh because that is what you do when someone says he can do the impossible. They laugh a little at God, and a lot *with* God—for God is laughing too. Then, with the smile still on his face, he gets busy doing what he does best—the unbelievable.

He changes a few things—beginning with their names. Abram, the father of one, will now be Abraham, the father of a multitude. Sarai, the barren one, will now be Sarah, the mother.

But their names aren't the only things God changes. He changes their minds. He changes their faith. He changes the number of their tax deductions. He changes the way they define the word *impossible*.

But most of all, he changes Sarah's attitude about trusting God. Were she to hear Jesus' statement about being poor in spirit, she could give a testimony: "He's right. I do things my way, I get a head-ache. I let God take over, I get a son. You try to figure that out. All I know is I am the first lady in town to pay her pediatrician with a Social Security check."

Two thousand years later, here's another testimony[2]:

"The last thing I wanted to do was fish. But that was exactly what Jesus wanted to do. I had fished all night. My arms ached. My eyes burned. My neck was sore. All I wanted was to go home and let my wife rub the knots out of my back.

"It had been a long night. I don't know how many times we had thrown that net into the blackness and heard it slap against the sea. I don't know how many times we had held the twine rope as the net sank into the water. All night we had waited for that bump, that tug, that jerk that would clue us to haul in the catch . . . but it had never come. At daybreak, I was ready to go home.

"Just as I was about to leave the beach, I noticed a crowd coming toward me. They were following a lanky fellow who walked with a broad swing and wide gait. He saw me and called my name. 'Morning, Jesus!' I called back. Though he was a hundred yards away, I could see his white smile. 'Quite a crowd, eh?' he yelled, motioning at the mass behind him. I nodded and sat down to watch.

"He stopped near the edge of the water and began to speak. Though I couldn't hear much, I could see a lot. I could see more and more people coming. With all the pressing and shoving, it's a wonder Jesus didn't get pushed down into the water. He was already knee-deep when he looked at me.

"I didn't have to think twice. He climbed into my boat, and John and I followed. We pushed out a bit. I leaned back against the bow, and Jesus began to teach.

"It seemed that half of Israel was on the beach. Men had left their work, women their household chores. I even recognized some priests. How they all listened! They scarcely moved, yet their eyes danced as if they were in some way seeing what they could be.

"When Jesus finished, he turned to me. I stood and had begun to pull anchor when he said, 'Push out into the deep, Peter. Let's fish.'

"I groaned. I looked at John. We were thinking the same thing. As long as he wanted to use the boat for a platform, that was fine. But to use it for a fishing boat—that was our territory. I started to tell this carpenter-teacher, 'You stick to preaching, and I'll stick to fishing.' But I was more polite: 'We worked all night. We didn't catch a thing.'

"He just looked at me. I looked at John. John was waiting for my cue . . .

"I wish I could say I did it because of love. I wish I could say I did it out of devotion. But I can't. All I can say is there is a time to question and a time to listen. So, as much with a grunt as with a prayer, we pushed out.

"With every stroke of the oar, I muttered. With every pull of the paddle, I grumbled. 'No way. No way. Impossible. I may not know much, but I know fishing. And all we're going to come back with are some wet nets.'

"The noise on the beach grew distant, and soon the only sound was the smack of the waves against the hull. Finally we cast anchor. I picked up the heavy netting, held it waist-high, and started to throw it. That's when I caught a glimpse of Jesus out of the corner of my eye. His expression stopped me in midmotion.

"He was leaning out over the edge of the boat, looking out into the water where I was about to throw the net. And, get this, he was smiling. A boyish grin pushed his cheeks high and turned his round eyes into half-moons—the kind of smile you see when a child gives a gift to a friend and watches as it is unwrapped.

"He noticed me looking at him, and he tried to hide the smile, but it persisted. It pushed at the corners of his mouth until a flash of teeth appeared. He had given me a gift and could scarcely contain himself as I opened it.

"'Boy, is he in for a disappointment,' I thought as I threw the net. It flew high, spreading itself against the blue sky and floating down until it flopped against the surface, then sank. I wrapped the rope once around my hand and sat back for the long wait.

"But there was no wait. The slack rope yanked taut and tried to pull me overboard. I set my feet against the side of the boat and yelled for help. John and Jesus sprang to my side.

"We got the net in just before it began to tear. I'd never seen such a catch. It was like plopping down a sack of rocks in the boat. We began to take in water. John screamed for the other boat to help us.

"It was quite a scene: four fishermen in two boats, knee-deep in fish, and one carpenter seated on our bow, relishing the pandemonium.

"That's when I realized who he was. And that's when I realized who I was: I was the one who told God what he couldn't do!

"'Go away from me, Lord; I'm a sinful man.' There wasn't anything else I could say.

"I don't know what he saw in me, but he didn't leave. Maybe he thought if I would let him tell me how to fish, I would let him tell me how to live.

"It was a scene I would see many times over the next couple of years—in cemeteries with the dead, on hillsides with the hungry, in storms with the frightened, on roadsides with the sick. The characters would change, but the theme wouldn't. When we would say, 'No way,' he would say, 'My way.' Then the ones who doubted would scramble to salvage the blessing. And the One who gave it would savor the surprise."

☙

"My power shows up best in weak people."[3]

God said those words. Paul wrote them down. God said he was looking for empty vessels more than strong muscles. Paul proved it.

Before he encountered Christ, Paul had been somewhat of a hero among the Pharisees. You might say he was their Wyatt Earp. He kept the law and order—or, better said, revered the Law and gave the orders. Good Jewish moms held him up as an example of a good Jewish boy. He was given the seat of honor at the Jerusalem Lions' Club Wednesday luncheon. He had a "Who's Who in Judaism" paperweight on his desk and was selected "Most Likely to Succeed" by his graduating class. He was quickly establishing himself as the heir apparent to his teacher, Gamaliel.

If there is such a thing as a religious fortune, Paul had it. He was a spiritual billionaire, born with one foot in heaven, and he knew it:

> If anyone ever had reason to hope that he could save himself, it would be I. If others could be saved by what they are, certainly I could! For I went through the Jewish initiation ceremony when I was eight days old, having been born into a pure-blooded Jewish home that was a branch of the old original Benjamin family. So I was a real Jew if there ever was one! What's more, I was a member of the Pharisees who demand the strictest obedience to every Jewish law and custom. And sincere? Yes, so much so that I greatly persecuted the Church; and I tried to obey every Jewish rule and regulation right down to the very last point.[4]

Blue-blooded and wild-eyed, this young zealot was hell-bent on keeping the kingdom pure—and that meant keeping the Christians out. He marched through the countryside like a general demanding that backslidden Jews salute the flag of the motherland or kiss their family and hopes good-bye.

All this came to a halt, however, on the shoulder of a highway. Equipped with subpoenas, handcuffs, and a posse, Paul was on his way to do a little personal evangelism in Damascus. That's when someone slammed on the stadium lights, and he heard the voice.

When he found out whose voice it was, his jaw hit the ground, and his body followed. He braced himself for the worst. He knew it was all over. He felt the noose around his neck. He smelled the flowers in the hearse. He prayed that death would be quick and painless.

But all he got was silence and the first of a lifetime of surprises.

He ended up bewildered and befuddled in a borrowed bedroom. God left him there a few days with scales on his eyes so thick that the only direction he could look was inside himself. And he didn't like what he saw.

He saw himself for what he really was—to use his own words, the worst of sinners.[5] A legalist. A killjoy. A bumptious braggart who claimed to have mastered God's code. A dispenser of justice who weighed salvation on a panscale.

That's when Ananias found him. He wasn't much to look at—haggard and groggy after three days of turmoil. Sarai wasn't much to look at either, nor was Peter. But what the three have in common says more than a volume of systematic theology. For when they gave up, God stepped in, and the result was a roller-coaster ride straight into the kingdom.

Paul was a step ahead of the rich young ruler. He knew better than to strike a deal with God. He didn't make any excuses; he just pleaded for mercy. Alone in the room with his sins on his conscience and blood on his hands, he asked to be cleansed.

Ananias's instructions to Paul are worth reading: "What are

you waiting for? Get up, be baptized and wash your sins away, calling on his name."[6]

He didn't have to be told twice. The legalist Saul was buried, and the liberator Paul was born. He was never the same afterwards. And neither was the world.

Stirring sermons, dedicated disciples, and six thousand miles of trails. If his sandals weren't slapping, his pen was writing. If he wasn't explaining the mystery of grace, he was articulating the theology that would determine the course of Western civilization.

All of his words could be reduced to one sentence. "We preach Christ crucified."[7] It wasn't that he lacked other sermon outlines; it was just that he couldn't exhaust the first one.

The absurdity of the whole thing kept him going. Jesus should have finished him on the road. He should have left him for the buzzards. He should have sent him to hell. But he didn't. He sent him to the lost.

Paul himself called it crazy. He described it with phrases like "stumbling block" and "foolishness," but chose in the end to call it "grace."[8]

And he defended his unquenchable loyalty by saying, "The love of Christ leaves [me] no choice."[9]

Paul never took a course in missions. He never sat in on a committee meeting. He never read a book on church growth. He was just inspired by the Holy Spirit and punch-drunk on the love that makes the impossible possible: salvation.

The message is gripping: Show a man his failures without Jesus, and the result will be found in the roadside gutter. Give a man religion without reminding him of his filth, and the result will be arrogance in a three-piece suit. But get the two in the same heart—get sin to meet Savior and Savior to meet sin—and the result just might be another Pharisee turned preacher who sets the world on fire.

☞

Four people: the rich young ruler, Sarah, Peter, Paul. A curious thread strings the four together—their names.

The final three had their names changed—Sarai to Sarah, Simon to Peter, Saul to Paul. But the first one, the young yuppie, is never mentioned by name.

Perhaps that's the clearest explanation of the first beatitude. The one who made a name for himself is nameless. But the ones who called on Jesus' name—and his name only—got new names and, even more, new life.

CHAPTER FIVE

———

The Prison of Pride

Blessed are those who mourn . . .

As Brazilian jail cells go this one wasn't too bad. There was a fan on the table. The twin beds each had a thin mattress and a pillow. There was a toilet and a sink.

No, it wasn't too bad. But, then again, I didn't have to stay.

Anibal did. He was there to stay.

Even more striking than his name (pronounced "uh-nee-ball") was the man himself. The tattooed anchor on his forearm symbolized his personality—cast-iron. His broad chest stretched his shirt. The slightest movement of his arm bulged his biceps. His face was as leathery in texture as it was in color. His glare could blister a foe. His smile was an explosion of white teeth.

But today the glare was gone and the smile was forced. Anibal wasn't on the street where he was the boss; he was in a jail where he was the prisoner.

He'd killed a man—a "neighborhood punk," as Anibal called him, a restless teenager who sold marijuana to the kids on the street and made a nuisance of himself with his mouth. One night the drug dealer had used his mouth one time too many and Anibal had decided to silence it. He'd left the crowded bar where the two of them had been arguing, gone home, taken a pistol out of a drawer, and walked back to the bar. Anibal had entered and called the boy's name. The drug dealer had turned around in time to take a bullet in the heart.

Anibal was guilty. Period. His only hope was that the judge would agree that he had done society a favor by getting rid of a neighborhood problem. He would be sentenced within the month.

I came to know Anibal through a Christian friend, Daniel. Anibal had lifted weights at Daniel's gym. Daniel had given Anibal a Bible and had visited him several times. This time Daniel took me with him to tell Anibal about Jesus.

Our study centered on the cross. We talked about guilt. We talked about forgiveness. The eyes of the murderer softened at the thought that the One who knows him best loves him most. His heart was touched as we discussed heaven, a hope that no executioner could take from him.

But as we began to discuss conversion, Anibal's face began to harden. The head that had leaned toward me in interest now straightened in caution. Anibal didn't like my statement that the first step in coming to God is an admission of guilt. He was uneasy with words like "I've been wrong" and "forgive me." Saying "I'm sorry" was out of character for him. He had never backed down before any man, and he wasn't about to do it now—even if the man were God.

In one final effort to pierce his pride, I asked him, "Don't you want to go to heaven?"

"Sure," he grunted.

"Are you ready?"

Earlier he might have boasted yes, but now he'd heard too many verses from the Bible. He knew better.

He stared at the concrete floor for a long time, meditating on the question. For a moment I thought his stony heart was cracking. For a second, it appeared that burly Anibal would for the first time admit his failures.

But I was wrong. The eyes that lifted to meet mine weren't tear-filled; they were angry. They weren't the eyes of a repentant prodigal; they were the eyes of an angry prisoner.

"All right," he shrugged. "I'll become one of your Christians. But don't expect me to change the way I live."

The conditional answer left my mouth bitter. "You don't draw up the rules," I told him. "It's not a contract that you negotiate before you sign. It's a gift—an undeserved gift! But to receive it, you have to admit that you need it."

"OK." He ran his thick fingers through his hair and stood up. "But don't expect to see me at church on Sundays."

I sighed. How many knocks in the head does a guy need before he'll ask for help?

As I watched Anibal pace back and forth in the tiny cell, I realized that his true prison was not made of bricks and mortar, but of pride. He was twice imprisoned. Once because of murder, and once because of stubbornness. Once by his country, and once by himself.

⌇

The prison of pride. For most of us it isn't as blatant as it was with Anibal, but the characteristics are the same. The upper lip is just as stiff. The chin ever protrudes upward, and the heart is just as hard.

A prison of pride is filled with self-made men and women determined to pull themselves up by their own bootstraps even if they land on their rear ends. It doesn't matter what they did or to whom they did it or where they will end up; it only matters that "I did it my way."

You've seen the prisoners. You've seen the alcoholic who won't admit his drinking problem. You've seen the woman who refuses to talk to anyone about her fears. You've seen the businessman who adamantly rejects help, even when his dreams are falling apart.

Perhaps to see such a prisoner all you have to do is look in the mirror.

"*If* we confess our sins, he is faithful and just . . ."[1] The biggest word in Scripture just might be that two-letter one, *if.* For confessing sins—admitting failure—is exactly what prisoners of pride refuse to do.

You know the lingo:

"Well, I may not be perfect, but I'm better than Hitler and certainly kinder than Idi Amin!"

"Me a sinner? Oh, sure, I get rowdy every so often, but I'm a pretty good ol' boy."

"Listen, I'm just as good as the next guy. I pay my taxes. I coach the Little League team. I even make donations to Red Cross. Why, God's probably proud to have somebody like me on his team."

Justification. Rationalization. Comparison. These are the tools of the jailbird. They sound good. They sound familiar. They even sound American. But in the kingdom, they sound hollow.

"Blessed are those who mourn . . ."

To mourn for your sins is a natural outflow of poverty of spirit. The second beatitude should follow the first. But that's not always the case. Many deny their weakness. Many know they are wrong, yet pretend they are right. As a result, they never taste the exquisite sorrow of repentance.

Of all the paths to joy, this one has to be the strangest. True blessedness, Jesus says, begins with deep sadness.

"Blessed are those who know they are in trouble and have enough sense to admit it."[2]

Joy through mourning? Freedom through surrender? Liberty through confession?

Want a model? Let me introduce you to one.

He was nitroglycerin; if you bumped him the wrong way, he blew up. He made a living with his hands and got in trouble with his mouth. In some ways, he had a lot in common with Anibal. If he had had a tattoo, it would have been a big, black anchor on his forearm. If they had had bumper stickers, his would have read, "I don't get mad; I get even."

He was a man among men on the Galilean sea. His family

called him Simon, but his master called him "Rocky." You know him as Peter.

And though he might not have known everything about self-control, he knew one thing about being a fisherman. He knew better than to get caught in a storm. . . .

And this night, Peter knows he is in trouble.

The winds roar down onto the Sea of Galilee like a hawk on a rat. Lightning zigzags across the black sky. The clouds vibrate with thunder. The rain taps, then pops, then slaps against the deck of the boat until everyone aboard is soaked and shaking. Ten-foot waves pick them up and slam them down again with bone-jarring force.

These drenched men don't look like a team of apostles who are only a decade away from changing the world. They don't look like an army that will march to the ends of the earth and reroute history. They don't look like a band of pioneers who will soon turn the world upside down. No, they look more like a handful of shivering sailors who are wondering if the next wave they ride will be their last.

And you can be sure of one thing. The one with the widest eyes is the one with the biggest biceps—Peter. He's seen these storms before. He's seen the wreckage and bloated bodies float to shore. He knows what the fury of wind and wave can do. And he knows that times like this are not times to make a name for yourself; they're times to get some help.

That is why, when he sees Jesus walking on the water toward the boat, he is the first to say, "Lord, if it's you . . . tell me to come to you on the water."[3]

Now, some say this statement is a simple request for verification. Peter, they suggest, wants to prove that the one they see is really Jesus and not just anyone who might be on a stroll across a storm-tossed sea in the middle of the night. (You can't be too careful, you know.)

So, Peter consults his notes, removes his glasses, clears his throat, and asks a question any good attorney would. "Ahem, Jesus, if you would kindly demonstrate your power and prove your divinity by calling me out on the water with you, I would be most appreciative."

I don't buy that. I don't think Peter is seeking clarification; I think he's trying to save his neck. He is aware of two facts: he's going down, and Jesus is staying up. And it doesn't take him too long to decide where he would rather be.

Perhaps a better interpretation of his request would be, "Jeeeeeeeesus. If that is you, then get me out of here!"

"Come on" is the invitation.

And Peter doesn't have to be told twice. It's not every day that you walk on water through waves that are taller than you are. But when faced with the alternative of sure death or possible life, Peter knows which one he wants.

The first few steps go well. But a few strides out onto the water, and he forgets to look to the One who got him there in the first place, and down he plunges.

At this point we see the major difference between Anibal and Peter—the difference between a man who hides his problem and one who admits it.

Anibal would be more concerned about his image than about his neck. He would prefer to go under rather than let his friends hear him ask for help. He would rather go down "his way" than get out "God's way."

Peter, on the other hand, knows better than to count the teeth in the mouth of a gift horse. He knows better than to bite the hand that can save him. His response may lack class—it probably wouldn't get him on the cover of *Gentleman's Quarterly* or even *Sports Illustrated*—but it gets him out of some deep water:

"Help me!"

And since Peter would rather swallow pride than water, a hand comes through the rain and pulls him up.

The message is clear.

As long as Jesus is one of many options, he is no option. As long as you can carry your burdens alone, you don't need a burden bearer. As long as your situation brings you no grief, you will receive no comfort. And as long as you can take him or leave him, you might as well leave him, because he won't be taken half-heartedly.

But when you mourn, when you get to the point of sorrow for your sins, when you admit that you have no other option but to cast all your cares on him, and when there is truly no other name that you can call, then cast all your cares on him, for he is waiting in the midst of the storm.

CHAPTER SIX

TOUCHES OF
TENDERNESS

. . . for they will be comforted.

BEING A PARENT IS BETTER THAN A THEOLOGY COURSE.

Two ten-year-old boys walked up to my five-year-old daughter on the bus yesterday, scowled at her, and demanded that she scoot over.

When I came home from work, she told me about it. "I wanted to cry, but I didn't. I just sat there—afraid."

My immediate impulse was to find out the names of the boys and punch their dads in the nose. But I didn't. I did what was more important. I pulled my little girl up into my lap and let her get lost inside my arms and told her not to worry about those old bullies because her daddy was here, and I'd make sure if any thugs ever got close to my princess they'd be taking their lives in their own hands, yessir.

And that was enough for Jenna. She bounded down and ran outside.

She came back a few minutes later, crying. Her elbow was scraped.

I picked her up and carried her into the bathroom for first aid. She tried to tell me what happened.

"I"—sniff, sniff—"was turning in circles"—sniff, sniff—"like a helicopter"—sniff, sniff—"and then I fell doaaaaawwwn," she wailed.

"It's gonna be OK," I said as I set her on the bathroom counter.

"Can I have a Band-Aid?"

"Of course."

"A big one?"

"The biggest."

"Really?"

I stretched the adhesive bandage over the scrape and held her arm up in the mirror so she could see her badge of courage.

"Wow. Can I go show Mommy?"

"Sure." I smiled.

And that was enough for Jenna.

"Daddy."

The voice was coming from another world—the world of the awake. I ignored it and stayed in the world of slumber.

"Daddy." The voice was insistent.

I opened one eye. Andrea, our three-year-old, was at the edge of my bed only a few inches from my face.

"Daddy, I'm scared."

I opened the other eye. It was three in the morning.

"What's wrong?"

"I need a fwashwight in my woom."

"What?"

"I need a fwashwight in my woom."

"Why?"

"'Cause it's dark."

I told her the lights were on. I told her the night light was on and the hall light was on.

"But Daddy," she objected, "what if I open my eyes and can't see anything?"

"Say that again."

"What if I open my eyes and can't see anything?"

Just as I was about to tell her that this was not the best time for questions on affliction, my wife interrupted. She explained to me that there was a power failure around midnight and Andrea must have awakened in the dark. No night light. No hall light. She had opened her eyes and had been unable to see anything. Just darkness.

Even the hardest of hearts would be touched by the thought of a child waking up in a darkness so black she couldn't find her way out of her room.

I climbed out of bed, picked Andrea up, got a flashlight out of the utility room, and carried her to her bed. All the while, I told her that Mom and Dad were here and that she didn't need to be afraid. I tucked her in and gave her a kiss.

And that was enough for Andrea.

My child's feelings are hurt. I tell her she's special. My child is injured. I do whatever it takes to make her feel better.

My child is afraid. I won't go to sleep until she is secure.

I'm not a hero. I'm not a superstar. I'm not unusual. I'm a parent. When a child hurts, a parent does what comes naturally. He helps.

And after I help, I don't charge a fee. I don't ask for a favor in return. When my child cries, I don't tell her to buck up, act tough, and keep a stiff upper lip. Nor do I consult a list and ask her why she is still scraping the same elbow or waking me up again.

I'm not brilliant, but you don't have to be to remember that a child is not an adult. You don't have to be a child psychologist to know that kids are "under construction." You don't have to have the wisdom of Solomon to realize that they didn't ask to be here in the first place and that spilled milk can be wiped up and broken plates can be replaced.

I'm not a prophet, nor the son of one, but something tells me that in the whole scheme of things the tender moments described above are infinitely more valuable than anything I do in front of a computer screen or congregation. Something tells me that the moments of comfort I give my child are a small price to pay for the joy of someday seeing my daughter do for her daughter what her dad did for her.

Moments of comfort from a parent. As a father, I can tell you they are the sweetest moments in my day. They come naturally. They come willingly. They come joyfully.

If all of that is true, if I know that one of the privileges of fatherhood is to comfort a child, then why am I so reluctant to let my heavenly Father comfort me?

Why do I think he wouldn't want to hear about my problems? ("They are puny compared to people starving in India.")

Why do I think he is too busy for me? ("He's got a whole universe to worry about.")

Why do I think he's tired of hearing the same old stuff?

Why do I think he groans when he sees me coming?

Why do I think he consults his list when I ask for forgiveness and asks, "Don't you think you're going to the well a few too many times on this one?"

Why do I think I have to speak a holy language around him that I don't speak with anyone else?

Why do I think he won't do in a heartbeat to the Father of Lies what I thought about doing to the fathers of those bullies on the bus?

Do I think he was just being poetic when he asked me if the birds of the air and the grass of the field have a worry? (No sir.) And if they don't, why do I think I will? (Duh. . . .)[1]

Why do I not take him seriously when he questions, "If you, then, though you are evil, know how to give good gifts to your children, how much more will your Father in heaven give good gifts to those who ask him!"[2]

Why don't I let my Father do for me what I am more than willing to do for my own children?

I'm learning, though. Being a parent is better than a course on theology. Being a father is teaching me that when I am criticized, injured, or afraid, there is a Father who is ready to comfort me.

There is a Father who will hold me until I'm better, help me until I can live with the hurt, and who won't go to sleep when I'm afraid of waking up and seeing the dark.

Ever.

And that's enough.

CHAPTER SEVEN

THE GLORY IN
THE ORDINARY

Blessed are the meek . . .

THERE IS ONE WORD THAT DESCRIBES THE NIGHT HE CAME—
ordinary.

The sky was ordinary. An occasional gust stirred the leaves and chilled the air. The stars were diamonds sparkling on black velvet. Fleets of clouds floated in front of the moon.

It was a beautiful night—a night worth peeking out your bedroom window to admire—but not really an unusual one. No reason to expect a surprise. Nothing to keep a person awake. An ordinary night with an ordinary sky.

The sheep were ordinary. Some fat. Some scrawny. Some with barrel bellies. Some with twig legs. Common animals. No fleece made of gold. No history makers. No blue-ribbon winners. They were simply sheep—lumpy, sleeping silhouettes on a hillside.

And the shepherds. Peasants they were. Probably wearing all the clothes they owned. Smelling like sheep and looking just as woolly. They were conscientious, willing to spend the night with their flocks. But you won't find their staffs in a museum nor their writings in a library. No one asked their opinion on social justice or the application of the Torah. They were nameless and simple.

An ordinary night with ordinary sheep and ordinary shepherds. And were it not for a God who loves to hook an "extra" on the front of the ordinary, the night would have gone unnoticed. The sheep would have been forgotten, and the shepherds would have slept the night away.

But God dances amidst the common. And that night he did a waltz.

The black sky exploded with brightness. Trees that had been shadows jumped into clarity. Sheep that had been silent became a chorus of curiosity. One minute the shepherd was dead asleep, the next he was rubbing his eyes and staring into the face of an alien.

The night was ordinary no more.

The angel came in the night because that is when lights are best seen and that is when they are most needed. God comes into the common for the same reason.

His most powerful tools are the simplest.

Consider the rod of Moses.[1] By this time in his life, Moses had been a shepherd as long as he had been a prince, and he'd grown accustomed to it. Herding sheep wasn't as lively as living with Egyptian royalty, but it had its moments, especially the moment God spoke to him through a burning bush that didn't burn up. God announced that Moses was his man to deliver the Israelites. Moses wasn't convinced he was the one for the job. God said that who Moses was didn't matter; what mattered was who God was. And God set out to demonstrate.

"Moses," spoke the voice from the bush, "throw down your staff."

Moses, who had walked this mountain for forty years, was not comfortable with the command.

"God, you know a lot about a lot of things, but you may not know that out here, well, you just don't go around throwing down your staff. You never know when . . ."

"Throw it down, Moses."

Moses threw it down. The rod became a snake, and Moses began to run.

"Moses!"

The old shepherd stopped.

"Pick up the snake."

Moses peered over his shoulder, first at the snake and then the bush, and then he gave the most courageous response he could muster.

"What?"

"Pick up the snake . . . by the tail." (God had to be smiling at this point.)

"God, I don't mean to object. I mean, you know a lot of things, but out here in the desert, well, you don't pick up snakes too often, and you *never* pick up snakes by the tail."

"Moses!"

"Yessir."

Just as Moses' hand touched the squirmy scales of the snake, it hardened. And Moses lifted up the rod. The same rod he would lift up in Pharaoh's court. The same rod he would lift up to divide the water and guide two million people through a desert. The rod that would remind Moses that if God can make a stick become a snake, then become a stick again—then perhaps he can do something with stubborn hearts and a stiff-necked people.

Perhaps he can do something with the common.

Or consider another shepherd from Bethlehem.[2]

There are certain things anyone knows not to do. You don't try to lasso a tornado. You don't fight a lion with a toothpick. You don't sneeze into the wind. You don't go bear hunting with a cork gun. And you don't send a shepherd boy to battle a giant.

You don't, that is, unless you are out of options. Saul was. And it is when we are out of options that we are most ready for God's surprises.

Was Saul ever surprised!

The king tried to give David some equipment. "What do you want, boy? Shield? Sword? Grenades? Rifles? A helicopter? We'll make a Rambo out of you."

David had something else in mind. Five smooth stones and an ordinary leather sling.

The soldiers gasped. Saul sighed. Goliath jeered.

David swung. And God made his point. "Anyone who underestimates what God can do with the ordinary has rocks in his head."

Or what about the blind man Jesus and the disciples discovered?[3]

The followers thought he was a great theological case study.

"Why do you think he's blind?" one asked.

"He must have sinned."

"No, it's his folks' fault."

"Jesus, what do you think? Why is he blind?"

"He's blind to show what God can do."

The apostles knew what was coming; they had seen this look in Jesus' eyes before. They knew what he was going to do, but they didn't know how he was going to do it. "Lightning? Thunder? A shout? A clap of the hands?" They all watched.

Jesus began to work his mouth a little. The onlookers stared. "What is he doing?" He moved his jaw as if he were chewing on something.

Some of the people began to get restless. Jesus just chewed. His jaw rotated around until he had what he wanted. Spit. Ordinary saliva.

If no one said it, somebody had to be thinking it: "Yuk!"

Jesus spat on the ground, stuck his finger into the puddle, and stirred. Soon it was a mud pie, and he smeared some of the mud across the blind man's eyes.

The same One who'd turned a stick into a scepter and a pebble into a missile now turned saliva and mud into a balm for the blind.

Once again, the mundane became majestic. Once again the dull became divine, the humdrum holy. Once again God's power was seen not through the ability of the instrument, but through its availability.

"Blessed are the meek," Jesus explained. Blessed are the available. Blessed are the conduits, the tunnels, the tools. Deliriously joyful are the ones who believe that if God has used sticks, rocks, and spit to do his will, then he can use us.

We would do well to learn a lesson from the rod, the rock, and the saliva. They didn't complain. They didn't question God's wisdom. They didn't suggest an alternative plan. Perhaps the reason the Father has used so many inanimate objects for his mission is that they don't tell him how to do his job!

It's like the story of the barber who became an artist. When asked why he changed professions, he replied, "A canvas doesn't tell me how to make it beautiful."

Neither do the meek.

That's why the announcement went first to the shepherds. They didn't ask God if he was sure he knew what he was doing. Had the angel gone to the theologians, they would have first consulted their commentaries. Had he gone to the elite, they would have looked around to see if anyone was watching. Had he gone to the successful, they would have first looked at their calendars.

So he went to the shepherds. Men who didn't have a reputation to protect or an ax to grind or a ladder to climb. Men who didn't know enough to tell God that angels don't sing to sheep and that messiahs aren't found wrapped in rags and sleeping in a feed trough.

A small cathedral outside Bethlehem marks the supposed birth-place of Jesus. Behind a high altar in the church is a cave, a little cavern lit by silver lamps.

You can enter the main edifice and admire the ancient church. You can also enter the quiet cave where a star embedded in the floor recognizes the birth of the King. There is one stipulation, however. You have to stoop. The door is so low you can't go in standing up.

The same is true of the Christ. You can see the world standing tall, but to witness the Savior, you have to get on your knees.

So . . .

> while the theologians were sleeping
>> and the elite were dreaming
>>> and the successful were snoring,
>>>> the meek were kneeling.

They were kneeling before the One only the meek will see. They were kneeling in front of Jesus.

CHAPTER EIGHT

THE BANDIT OF JOY

. . . for they will inherit the earth.

HE WAS A PROFESSIONAL THIEF. HIS NAME STIRRED FEAR AS the desert wind stirs tumbleweeds. He terrorized the Wells Fargo stage line for thirteen years, roaring like a tornado in and out of the Sierra Nevadas, spooking the most rugged frontiersmen. In journals from San Francisco to New York, his name became synonymous with the danger of the frontier.

During his reign of terror between 1875 and 1883, he is credited with stealing the bags and the breath away from twenty-nine different stagecoach crews. And he did it all without firing a shot.

His weapon was his reputation. His ammunition was intimidation.

A hood hid his face. No victim ever saw him. No artist ever sketched his features. No sheriff could ever track his trail. He never fired a shot or took a hostage.

He didn't have to. His presence was enough to paralyze.

Black Bart. A hooded bandit armed with a deadly weapon.

He reminds me of another thief—one who's still around. You know him. Oh, you've never seen his face, either. You couldn't describe his voice or sketch his profile. But when he's near, you know it in a heartbeat.

If you've ever been in the hospital, you've felt the leathery brush of his hand against yours.

If you've ever sensed someone was following you, you've felt his cold breath down your neck.

If you've awakened late at night in a strange room, it was his husky whisper that stole your slumber.

You know him.

It was this thief who left your palms sweaty as you went for the job interview.

It was this con man who convinced you to swap your integrity for popularity.

And it was this scoundrel who whispered in your ear as you left the cemetery, "You may be next."

He's the Black Bart of the soul. He doesn't want your money. He doesn't want your diamonds. He won't go after your car. He wants something far more precious. He wants your peace of mind—your joy.

His name?

Fear.

His task is to take your courage and leave you timid and

trembling. His *modus operandi* is to manipulate you with the mysterious, to taunt you with the unknown. Fear of death, fear of failure, fear of God, fear of tomorrow—his arsenal is vast. His goal? To create cowardly, joyless souls.

He doesn't want you to make the journey to the mountain. He figures if he can rattle you enough, you will take your eyes off the peaks and settle for a dull existence in the flatlands.

⌒

A legend from India tells about a mouse who was terrified of cats until a magician agreed to transform him into a cat. That resolved his fear . . . until he met a dog, so the magician changed him into a dog. The mouse-turned-cat-turned-dog was content until he met a tiger—so, once again, the magician changed him into what he feared. But when the tiger came complaining that he had met a hunter, the magician refused to help. "I will make you into a mouse again, for though you have the body of a tiger, you still have the heart of a mouse."

Sound familiar? How many people do you know who have built a formidable exterior, only to tremble inside with fear? We tackle our anxieties by taking on the appearance of a tiger. We face our fears with force. Military power, security systems, defense strategy—all reflect a conviction that muscle creates security.

Or if we don't use force, we try other methods. We stockpile wealth. We seek security in things. We cultivate fame and seek status.

But do these approaches work? Can power, possessions, or popularity really deliver us from our fears?

If power could, then Joseph Stalin should have been fearless. Instead, this infamous Russian premier was afraid to go bed. He had seven different bedrooms. Each could be locked as tightly as a safe. In order to foil any would-be assassins, he slept in a different one each night. Five chauffeur-driven limousines transported him wherever he went, each with curtains closed so no one would know which contained Stalin. So deep-seated were his apprehensions that he employed a servant whose sole task was to monitor and protect his tea bags.[1]

If possessions conquered fear, the late billionaire Howard Hughes would have been fearless. But you probably know his story. His distrust of people and his paranoia of germs led this billionaire to Mexico, where he died a lonely death as a cadaverous hermit with a belly-length beard and corkscrew fingernails.[2]

What about popularity? Beatle John Lennon's fame as a singer, songwriter, and pop icon made him a household word, but his fears brought him misery. His biographers describe him as a frightened man, unwilling to sleep with the lights off and afraid to touch anything because of its filth.[3]

Though Stalin, Hughes, and Lennon are extreme cases, they are indicative ones. "Though you have the body of a tiger, you still have the heart of a mouse."

Parallel their stories with the life of a little-known but gutsy young man named Paul Keating. On a cold night in February 1980, twenty-seven-year-old Keating was walking home in Manhattan's Greenwich Village when he saw two armed muggers robbing a college student. Keating, a gentle, much-admired photographer for *Time* magazine, had every reason to avoid trouble. He didn't know the student. No one knew he saw the crime. He was outnumbered.

He had nothing to gain and much to lose by taking the risk, and yet he jumped on the muggers. The victim escaped and ran to a nearby deli to call for help. Moments later, two shots cracked the night, and the muggers fled. Paul Keating was found dead on the pavement.

The city of New York posthumously awarded him a medal of heroism. I think you'll agree with the commentary offered by Mayor Edward Koch at the ceremony: "Nobody was watching Paul Keating on the street that night. Nobody made him step forward in the time of crisis. He did it because of who he was."[4]

Well put.

Courage is an outgrowth of who we are. Exterior supports may temporarily sustain, but only inward character creates courage.

And it is those inward convictions that Jesus is building in the Beatitudes. Remember, Matthew 5 is not a list of proverbs or a compilation of independent sayings, but rather a step-by-step description of how God rebuilds the believer's heart.

The first step is to ask for help—to become "poor in spirit" and admit our need for a Savior.

The next step is sorrow: "Blessed are those who mourn . . ." Those who mourn are those who know they are wrong and say they are sorry. No excuses. No justification. Just tears.

The first two steps are admittance of inadequacy and repentance for pride. The next step is the one of renewal: "Blessed are the meek. . . ." Realization of weakness leads to the source of strength— God. And renewal comes when we become meek—when we give our lives to God to be his tool.

The first two beatitudes pass us through the fire of purification; the third places us in the hands of the Master.

The result of this process? Courage: "They shall inherit the earth." No longer shall the earth and its fears dominate us, for we follow the One who dominates the earth.

⌒

Could you use some courage? Are you backing down more than you are standing up? If so, let the Master lead you up the mountain again. Let him remind you why you should "fear not." Listen to the time Jesus scattered the butterflies out of the stomachs of his nervous disciples and see if his words help you.[5]

We need to remember that the disciples were common men given a compelling task. Before they were the stained-glassed saints in the windows of cathedrals, they were somebody's next-door-neighbors trying to make a living and raise a family. They weren't cut from theological cloth or raised on supernatural milk. But they were an ounce more devoted than they were afraid and, as a result, did some extraordinary things.

They would have done nothing, however, had they not learned to face their fears. Jesus knew that. That is why he spoke his words of courage.

The disciples are being sent out on their own. For a limited time they will go into the cities and do what Jesus has done—but without Jesus. Jesus assembles them to give them the final instructions. Perhaps the disciples look nervous, for they have reason to be nervous. What Jesus tells them would raise the pulse rate of the stoutest heart.

First Jesus tells them not to take any extra money or extra clothing on their journey.

"No money?"

Then he assures them that they are being sent out "like sheep among wolves."

"Uh, what do you mean, Jesus?"

His answer is not reassuring. He tells them they will be taken before the authorities (uh-oh), flogged (ouch), and arrested (groan).

And it gets worse before it gets better.

Jesus goes on to describe the impact their mission will have on people: "Brother will betray brother to death, and a father his child; children will rebel against their parents and have them put to death. All men will hate you because of me, but he who stands firm to the end will be saved."[6]

Some eyes duck. Some eyes widen. Someone swallows. Feet shift. A brow is wiped. And though no one says it, you know someone is thinking, "Is it too late to get out of this?"

That's the setting for Jesus' paragraph on courage. Three times in five verses[7] he says, "Do not be afraid." Read the words and see his call and cause for courage. See the reason you should sleep well tonight:

"So do not be afraid of them. There is nothing concealed that will not be disclosed, or hidden that will not be made known."[8]

On the surface, those words would seem like a reason for panic rather than a source of peace. Who of us would like to have our secret thoughts made public? Who would want our private sins published? Who would get excited over the idea that every wrong deed we've ever done will be announced to everyone?

You're right, no one would. But we're told over and over that such a thing *will* happen:

Nothing in all creation is hidden from God's sight. Everything is uncovered and laid bare before the eyes of him to whom we must give account.

He reveals deep and hidden things;
   he knows what lies in darkness,
      and light dwells with him.

But I tell you that men will have to give account on the day of judgment for every careless word they have spoken.

You have set our iniquities before you,
   our secret sins in the light of your presence.

He will bring to light what is hidden in darkness and will expose the motives of men's hearts.[9]

To think of the disclosure of my hidden heart conjures up emotions of shame, humiliation, and embarrassment in me. There are things I've done that I want no one to know. There are thoughts I've thought I would never want to be revealed. So why does Jesus point to the day of revelation as a reason for *courage*? How can I take strength in what should be a moment of anguish?

The answer is found in Romans 2:16. Let out a sigh of relief as you underline the last three words of the verse: "This will take place on the day when God will judge men's secrets *through Jesus Christ*" (emphasis mine).

Did you see it? Jesus is the screen through which God looks when he judges our sins. Now read another chorus of verses and focus on their promise:

Therefore, there is now no condemnation for those who are in Christ Jesus.

[God] justifies those who have faith in Jesus.

Through him everyone who believes is justified from everything.

For I will forgive their wickedness
    and will remember their sins no more.

For you died, and your life is now hidden with Christ in God.[10]

If you are in Christ, these promises are not only a source of joy. They are also the foundations of true courage. You are guaranteed that your sins will be filtered through, hidden in, and screened out by the sacrifice of Jesus. When God looks at you, he doesn't see you; he sees the One who surrounds you. That means that failure is not a concern for you. Your victory is secure. How could you not be courageous?

Picture it this way. Imagine that you are an ice skater in competition. You are in first place with one more round to go. If you perform well, the trophy is yours. You are nervous, anxious, and frightened.

Then, only minutes before your performance, your trainer rushes to you with the thrilling news: "You've already won! The judges tabulated the scores, and the person in second place can't catch you. You are too far ahead."

Upon hearing that news, how will you feel? Exhilarated!

And how will you skate? Timidly? Cautiously? Of course not. How about courageously and confidently? You bet you will. You will do your best because the prize is yours. You will skate like a champion because that is what you are! You will hear the applause of victory.

Hence, these words from Hebrews: "Therefore, brothers, since we have *confidence* to enter the Most Holy Place by the blood of Jesus . . . let us draw near to God with a sincere heart in *full assurance* of faith."[11]

The point is clear: the truth will triumph. The Father of truth will win, and the followers of truth will be saved.

As a result, Jesus says, don't be afraid:

What I tell you in the dark, speak in the daylight; what is whispered in your ear, proclaim from the roofs. Do not be afraid of those who kill the body but cannot kill the soul. Rather, be afraid of the One who can destroy both soul and body in hell.[12]

Earthly fears are no fears at all. All the mystery is revealed. The final destination is guaranteed. Answer the big question of eternity, and the little questions of life fall into perspective.

And by the way, remember Black Bart? As it turns out, he wasn't anything to be afraid of, either. When the hood came off, there was nothing to fear. When the authorities finally tracked down the thief, they didn't find a bloodthirsty bandit from Death Valley; they found a mild-mannered druggist from Decatur, Illinois. The man the papers pictured storming through the mountains on horseback was, in reality, so afraid of horses he rode to and from his robberies in a buggy. He was Charles E. Boles—the bandit who never once fired a shot, because he never once loaded his gun.[13]

Any false hoods in your world?

CHAPTER NINE

A Satisfied Thirst

Blessed are those who hunger and thirst for righteousness . . .

Mommy, I'm so thirsty. I want a drink."

Susanna Petroysan heard her daughter's pleas, but there was nothing she could do. She and four-year-old Gayaney were trapped beneath tons of collapsed concrete and steel. Beside them in the darkness lay the body of Susanna's sister-in-law, Karine, one of the fifty-five thousand victims of the worst earthquake in the history of Soviet Armenia.

Calamity never knocks before it enters, and this time, it had torn down the door.

Susanna had gone to Karine's house to try on a dress. It was December 7, 1988, at 11:30 a.m. The quake hit at 11:41. She had just removed the dress and was clad in stockings and a slip when the fifth-floor apartment began to shake. Susanna grabbed her daughter but had taken only a few steps before the floor opened up and they tumbled in. Susanna, Gayaney, and Karine fell into the basement with the nine-story apartment house crumbling around them.

"Mommy, I need a drink. Please give me something."

There was nothing for Susanna to give.

She was trapped flat on her back. A concrete panel eighteen inches above her head and a crumpled water pipe above her shoulders kept her from standing. Feeling around in the darkness, she found a twenty-four-ounce jar of blackberry jam that had fallen into the basement. She gave the entire jar to her daughter to eat. It was gone by the second day.

"Mommy, I'm so thirsty."

Susanna knew she would die, but she wanted her daughter to live. She found a dress, perhaps the one she had come to try on, and made a bed for Gayaney. Though it was bitter cold, she took off her stockings and wrapped them around the child to keep her warm.

The two were trapped for eight days.

Because of the darkness, Susanna lost track of time. Because of the cold, she lost the feeling in her fingers and toes. Because of her inability to move, she lost hope. "I was just waiting for death."

She began to hallucinate. Her thoughts wandered. A merciful sleep occasionally freed her from the horror of her entombment, but the sleep would be brief. Something always awakened her: the cold, the hunger, or—most often—the voice of her daughter.

"Mommy, I'm thirsty."

At some point in that eternal night, Susanna had an idea. She remembered a television program about an explorer in the Arctic who was dying of thirst. His comrade slashed open his hand and gave his friend his blood.

"I had no water, no fruit juice, no liquids. It was then I remembered I had my own blood."

Her groping fingers, numb from the cold, found a piece of shattered glass. She sliced open her left index finger and gave it to her daughter to suck.

The drops of blood weren't enough. "Please, Mommy, some more. Cut another finger." Susanna has no idea how many times she cut herself. She only knows that if she hadn't, Gayaney would have died. Her blood was her daughter's only hope.

꩜

"This cup is the new covenant in my blood," Jesus explained, holding up the wine.[1]

The claim must have puzzled the apostles. They had been taught the story of the Passover wine. It symbolized the lamb's blood that the Israelites, enslaved long ago in Egypt, had painted on the doorposts of their homes. That blood had kept death from their homes and saved their firstborn. It had helped deliver them from the clutches of the Egyptians.

For thousands of generations the Jews had observed the Passover by sacrificing the lambs. Every year the blood would be poured, and every year the deliverance would be celebrated.

The law called for spilling the blood of a lamb. That would be enough.

It would be enough to fulfill the law. It would be enough to satisfy the command. It would be enough to justify God's justice.

But it would not be enough to take away sin.

"Because it is impossible for the blood of bulls and goats to take away sins."[2]

Sacrifices could offer temporary solutions, but only God could offer the eternal one.

So he did.

Beneath the rubble of a fallen world, he pierced his hands. In the wreckage of a collapsed humanity, he ripped open his side. His children were trapped, so he gave his blood.

It was all he had. His friends were gone. His strength was waning. His possessions had been gambled away at his feet. Even his Father had turned his head. His blood was all he had. But his blood was all it took.

"If anyone is thirsty," Jesus once said, "let him come to me and drink."[3]

Admission of thirst doesn't come easy for us. False fountains pacify our cravings with sugary swallows of pleasure. But there comes a time when pleasure doesn't satisfy. There comes a dark hour in every life when the world caves in and we are left trapped in the rubble of reality, parched and dying.

Some would rather die than admit it. Others admit it and escape death.

"God, I need help."

So the thirsty come. A ragged lot we are, bound together by broken dreams and collapsed promises. Fortunes that were never made. Families that were never built. Promises that were never kept. Wide-eyed children trapped in the basement of our own failures.

And we are very thirsty.

Not thirsty for fame, possessions, passion, or romance. We've drunk from those pools. They are salt water in the desert. They don't quench—they kill.

"Blessed are those who hunger and thirst for righteousness . . ."

Righteousness. That's it. That's what we are thirsty for. We're thirsty for a clean conscience. We crave a clean slate. We yearn for a fresh start. We pray for a hand which will enter the dark cavern of our world and do for us the one thing we can't do for ourselves—make us right again.[4]

~

"Mommy, I'm so thirsty," Gayaney begged.

"It was then I remembered I had my own blood," Susanna explained.

And the hand was cut, and the blood was poured, and the child was saved.

"God, I'm so thirsty," we pray.

"It is my blood, the blood of the new agreement," Jesus stated, "shed to set many free from their sins."[5]

And the hand was pierced,
　　and the blood was poured,
　　　　and the children are saved.

CHAPTER TEN

LIFE IN THE PITS

. . . for they will be filled.

I TOOK MY TWO OLDEST DAUGHTERS TO SEA WORLD RECENTLY.
My wife was out of town, so Jenna, Andrea, and I went to spend the
day watching the dolphins dip, the walruses waddle, and the pen-
guins paddle.

We had a great day. Hot dogs. Ice cream. Stuffed whales. Toys,
toys, and toys. The girls know their dad is a pushover for a thirteen-
letter "Pleeeeeeeease." I should have known better. The average
interest in amusement park memorabilia is twelve minutes and
thirty-two seconds. Then it is, "Daddy, can you hold this? It's too
heavy."

"Now, I told you not to buy it if you couldn't hold on to it."

"Pleeeeeeeease."

So by the end of the day I was carrying two pen-and-pencil sets, one set of sunglasses, an inflated penguin, a shark's tooth (complete with shark), a life-sized stuffed version of Shamu the killer whale, six balloons, and a live turtle. (OK, I'm exaggerating; there were only five balloons.) Add to that the heat, the rash from getting splashed with salt water, and the Eskimo Pie that melted down my shirt, and I was ready for a break.

That's why I was glad to see the plastic ball pit. This one activity is enough to convince you to keep your season pass current. It's a large, covered, shady, cool, soothing pavilion. Under the awning is a four-foot-deep pit the size of a backyard pool. But rather than being filled with water, it is loaded with balls—thousands and thousands of plastic, colorful, lightweight balls.

In the center of the pit is a sort of table with holes through which blow jets of air. Kids climb through the pit, grab balls, place them over the holes, and "Whee!"—up fly the balls.

The greatest part of the pit is the parents' area. While the kids roll and romp in the balls, the parents sit on the carpeted floor next to the pit and rest.

My oldest daughter, Jenna, did great. She dove in and made a beeline to the table.

Three-year-old Andrea, however, had a few difficulties. As soon as she took one step into the pit, she filled her arms with balls.

Now, it is hard enough to walk through the waist-high pit of balls with your arms spread to keep your balance. It is *impossible* to do it with your arms full.

Andrea took a step and fell. She tried to wrestle her way up without releasing the balls. She couldn't. She began to cry. I walked over to the edge of the pit.

"Andrea," I said gently, "let go of the balls, and you can walk."

"No!" she screamed, wiggling and submerging herself beneath the balls. I reached in and pulled her up. She was still clutching her armful of treasures.

"Andrea," her wise, patient father said, "if you'll let the balls go, you'll be able to walk. Besides, there are plenty of balls near the table."

"No!"

She took two steps and fell again.

Parents aren't supposed to go into the pit. I tried to reach her from the edge, but I couldn't. She was somewhere under the balls, so I spoke toward the area where she had fallen. "Andrea, let go of the balls so you can get up."

I saw a movement under the balls. "Nooo!!"

"Andrea," spoke her slightly agitated father. "You could get up if you would let go of . . ."

"Nooooo!!!!!"

"Jenna, come here and help your sister up."

By now the other parents were beginning to look at me. Jenna waded through the balls toward her little sister. She reached down into the pit and tried to help Andrea onto her feet. Jenna wasn't strong enough, and Andrea couldn't help because she was still clutching the same balls she had grabbed when she first stepped into the pit.

Jenna straightened up and shook her head at me. "I can't get her up, Daddy."

"Andrea," her increasingly irritated father said loudly, "let go of the balls so you can get up!"

The cry from beneath the balls was muffled, but distinct. "Nooooo!!!!!"

"Great," I thought to myself. "She's got what she wants, and she's going to hold on to it if it kills her."

"Jenna," her visibly angered father said sternly. "Take those balls away from your sister."

Down Jenna dove, digging through the balls like a puppy digging through the dirt. I knew she had found her little sister and that the two were engaged in mortal combat when waves of balls began to move on the surface of the pit.

By now the other parents were whispering and pointing. I looked forlornly at the employee who was monitoring the pit. I didn't even have to say a word. "Go on in," he told me.

I waded through the balls to my two angels, broke the death-locks they had on each other, put one under each arm, and carried them to the center of the pit. I dropped them next to the table (all the other kids scrambled away when they saw me coming). Then I marched back to the side of the pit and sat down.

As I watched the girls play with the balls, I asked myself, "What is it that makes children immobilize themselves by clutching toys so tightly?"

I winced as a response surfaced. "Whatever it is, they learned it from their parents."

Andrea's determination to hold those balls is nothing compared to the vice-grips we put on life. If you think Jenna's job of taking the balls away from Andrea was tough, try prying our fingers away from our earthly treasures. Try taking a retirement account away from a fifty-five-year-old. Or try convincing a yuppie to give up her BMW. Or test your luck on a clotheshorse and his or her wardrobe. The way we clutch our possessions and our pennies, you'd think we couldn't live without them.

Ouch.

⌒

Jesus' promise is comprehensive: "Blessed are those who hunger and thirst for righteousness, for they will be filled."

We usually get what we hunger and thirst for. The problem is, the treasures of earth don't satisfy. The promise is, the treasures of heaven do.

Blessed are those, then, who hold their earthly possessions in open palms. Blessed are those who, if everything they own were taken from them, would be, at most, inconvenienced, because their true wealth is elsewhere. Blessed are those who are totally dependent upon Jesus for their joy.

"Andrea," her father pleaded, "there are more than enough balls to play with at the table. Concentrate on walking."

"Max," the heavenly Father pleads, "there are more riches than you could ever dream at the banquet table. Concentrate on walking."

Our resistance to our Father is just as childish as Andrea's. God, for our own good, tries to loosen our grip from something that will cause us to fall. But we won't let go.

"No, I won't give up my weekend rendezvous for eternal joy."

"Trade a life addicted to drugs and alcohol for a life of peace and a promise of heaven? Are you kidding?"

"I don't want to die. I don't want a new body. I want this one. I don't care if it is fat, balding, and destined to decay. I want this body."

And there we lie, submerged in the pits, desperately clutching the very things that cause us grief.

It's a wonder the Father doesn't give up.

CHAPTER ELEVEN

The Father in the Face of the Enemy

Blessed are the merciful, for they will be shown mercy.

MARCH 24, 1989. A COLD NIGHT OFF THE COAST OF ALASKA.
The captain of a tanker barked orders to a second mate. The orders were vague, the night was black, and the collision was disastrous. The tanker ship *Exxon Valdez* ran hard aground on Bligh Reef, dumping eleven million gallons of crude oil into one of the most scenic bodies of water in the world. Petroleum blackened everything from the surface of the sea, to beaches, to otters, to sea gulls. Alaska was infuriated, and Exxon, the company which owned the tanker, was humiliated.

The collision, terrible as it was, was mild compared to the ones that occur daily in our relationships. You've been there. Someone doesn't meet your expectations. Promises go unfulfilled. Verbal pistols are drawn, and a round of words is fired.

The result? A collision of the hull of your heart against the reef of someone's actions. Precious energy escapes, coating the surface of your soul with the deadly film of resentment. A black blanket of bitterness darkens your world, dims your sight, sours your outlook, and suffocates your joy.

Do you have a hole in your heart?

Perhaps the wound is old. A parent abused you. A teacher slighted you. A mate betrayed you. A business partner bailed out, leaving you a choice of bills or bankruptcy.

And you are angry.

Or perhaps the wound is fresh. The friend who owes you money just drove by in a new car. The boss who hired you with promises of promotions has forgotten how to pronounce your name. Your circle of friends escaped on a weekend getaway, and you weren't invited. The children you raised seem to have forgotten you exist.

And you are hurt.

Part of you is broken, and the other part is bitter. Part of you wants to cry, and part of you wants to fight. The tears you cry are hot because they come from your heart, and there is a fire burning in your heart. It's the fire of anger. It's blazing. It's consuming. Its flames leap up under a steaming pot of revenge.

And you are left with a decision. "Do I put the fire out or heat it up? Do I get over it or get even? Do I release it or resent it? Do I let my hurts heal, or do I let hurt turn into hate?"

That's a good definition of resentment: Resentment is when you let your hurt become hate. Resentment is when you allow what is eating you to eat you up. Resentment is when you poke, stoke, feed, and fan the fire, stirring the flames and reliving the pain.

Resentment is the deliberate decision to nurse the offense until it becomes a black, furry, growling grudge.

Grudge is one of those words that defines itself. Its very sound betrays its meaning.

Say it slowly: "Grr-uuuud-ge."

It starts with a growl. "Grr . . ." Like a bear with bad breath coming out of hibernation or a mangy mongrel defending his bone in an alley. "Grrr . . ."

Being near a resentful person and petting a growling dog are equally enjoyable.

Don't you just love being next to people who are nursing a grudge? Isn't it a delight to listen to them sing their songs of woe? They are so optimistic! They are so full of hope. They are bubbling with life.

You know better. You know as well as I that if they are bubbling with anything it is anger. And if they are full of anything, it is poisonous barbs of condemnation for all the people who have hurt them. Grudge bearers and angry animals are a lot alike. Both are irritable. Both are explosive. Both can be rabid. Someone needs to make a sign that can be worn around the neck of the resentful: "Beware of the Grrrrudge Bearer."

Add an *M* to the second part of the word, and you will see

what grudge bearers throw. Mud. It's not enough to accuse; the other person's character must be attacked. It's insufficient to point a finger; a rifle must be aimed. Slander is slung. Names are called. Circles are drawn. Walls are built. And enemies are made.

Remove a *GR* from the word *grudge* and replace it with *SL* and you have the junk that grudge bearers trudge through. Sludge. Black, thick, ankle-deep resentment that steals the bounce from the step. No joyful skips through the meadows. No healthy hikes up the mountain. Just day after day of walking into the storm, shoulders bent against the wind, and feet dragging through all the muck life has delivered.

Is this the way you are coping with your hurts? Are you allowing your hurts to turn into hates? If so, ask yourself: Is it working? Has your hatred done you any good? Has your resentment brought you any relief, any peace? Has it granted you any joy?

Let's say you get even. Let's say you get him back. Let's say she gets what she deserves. Let's say your fantasy of fury runs its ferocious course and you return all your pain with interest. Imagine yourself standing over the corpse of the one you have hated. Will you now be free?

The writer of the following letter thought she would be. She thought her revenge would bring release. But she learned otherwise.

I caught my husband making love to another woman. He swore it would never happen again. He begged me to forgive him, but I could not—would not. I was so bitter and so incapable of swallowing my pride that I could think of nothing but revenge. I was going to make him pay and pay dearly. I'd have my pound of flesh.

I filed for divorce, even though my children begged me not to.

Even after the divorce, my husband tried for two years to win me back. I refused to have anything to do with him. He had struck first; now I was striking back. All I wanted was to make him pay.

Finally he gave up and married a lovely young widow with a couple of small children. He began rebuilding his life—without me.

I see them occasionally, and he looks so happy. They all do. And here I am—a lonely, old, miserable woman who allowed her selfish pride and foolish stubbornness to ruin her life.

Unfaithfulness is wrong. Revenge is bad. But the worst part of all is that, without forgiveness, bitterness is all that is left.

Resentment is the cocaine of the emotions. It causes our blood to pump and our energy level to rise.

But, also like cocaine, it demands increasingly larger and more frequent dosages. There is a dangerous point at which anger ceases to be an emotion and becomes a driving force. A person bent on revenge moves unknowingly further and further away from being able to forgive, for to be without the anger is to be without a source of energy.

That explains why the bitter complain to anyone who will listen. They want—they need—to have their fire fanned. That helps explain the existence of the KKK, the Skinheads, and other hate organizations. Members of these groups feed each other's anger.

And that is why the resentful often appear unreasonable. They are addicted to their bitterness. They don't want to surrender their anger, for to do so would be to surrender their reason to live.

Take bigotry from the racist, and what does he have left? Remove revenge from the heart of the zealot, and her life is empty. Extract chauvinism from the radical sexist, and what remains?

Resentment is like cocaine in another way, too. Cocaine can kill the addict. And anger can kill the angry.

It can kill physically. Chronic anger has been linked with elevated cholesterol, high blood pressure, and other deadly conditions. It can kill emotionally, in that it can raise anxiety levels and lead to depression.[1]

And it can be spiritually fatal, too. It shrivels the soul.

Hatred is the rabid dog that turns on its owner. Revenge is the raging fire that consumes the arsonist. Bitterness is the trap that snares the hunter.

And mercy is the choice that can set them all free.

"Blessed are the merciful," said Jesus on the mountain. Those who are merciful to others are the ones who are truly blessed. Why? Jesus answered the question: "They will be shown mercy."

The merciful, says Jesus, are shown mercy. They witness grace. They are blessed because they are testimonies to a greater goodness. Forgiving others allows us to see how God has forgiven us. The dynamic of giving grace is the key to understanding grace, for it is when we forgive others that we begin to feel what God feels.

Jesus told the story of a king who decided to close out all his accounts with those who worked for him.[2] He called in his debtors and told them to pay. One man owed an amount too great to return—a debt that could never be repaid. But when the king saw the man and heard his story, his heart went out to him, and he erased the debt.

As the man was leaving the palace grounds, he encountered a fellow employee who owed him a small sum. He grabbed the debtor and choked him, demanding payment. When the fellow begged for mercy, no mercy was granted. Instead, the one who had just been forgiven had his debtor thrown into jail.

When word of this got to the king, he became livid. And Jesus says, "In anger his master turned him over to the jailers to be tortured, until he should pay back all he owed."[3]

Could someone actually be forgiven a debt of millions and be unable to forgive a debt of hundreds? Could a person be set free and then imprison another?

You don't have to be a theologian to answer those questions; you only have to look in the mirror. Who among us has not begged God for mercy on Sunday and then demanded justice on Monday? Who hasn't served as a bottleneck instead of a conduit of God's love? Is there anyone who doesn't, at one time or the other, "show contempt for the riches of his [God's] kindness, tolerance and patience, not realizing that God's kindness leads you towards repentance?"[4]

Notice what God does when we calibrate our compassion. He turns us over to be tortured. Tortured by anger. Choked by bitterness. Consumed by revenge.

Such is the punishment for one who tastes God's grace but refuses to share it.

But for the one who tastes God's grace and then gives it to others, the reward is a blessed liberation. The prison door is thrown open, and the prisoner set free is yourself.

Earlier in the book I mentioned Daniel, a dear friend of mine in Brazil. (Daniel was the one who took me to meet Anibal in prison.)

Daniel is big. He used to make his living by lifting weights and teaching others to do the same. His scrapbook is colorful with ribbons and photos of him in his prime, striking the muscle-man pose and flexing the bulging arms.

The only thing bigger than Daniel's biceps is his heart. Let me tell you about a time his heart became tender.

Daniel was living in the southern city of Porto Alegre. He worked at a gym and dreamed of owning his own. The bank agreed to finance the purchase if he could find someone to cosign the note. His brother agreed.

They filled out all the applications and awaited the approval. Everything went smoothly, and Daniel soon received a call from the bank telling him he could come and pick up the check. As soon as he got off work, he went to the bank.

When the loan officer saw Daniel, he looked surprised and asked Daniel why he had come.

"To pick up the check," Daniel explained.

"That's funny," responded the banker. "Your brother was in here earlier. He picked up the money and used it to retire the mortgage on his house."

Daniel was incensed. He never dreamed his own brother would trick him like that. He stormed over to his brother's house and pounded on the door. The brother answered the door with his daughter in his arms. He knew Daniel wouldn't hit him if he was holding a child.

He was right. Daniel didn't hit him. But he promised his brother that if he ever saw him again he would break his neck.

Daniel went home, his big heart bruised and ravaged by the trickery of his brother. He had no other choice but to go back to the gym and work to pay off the debt.

A few months later, Daniel met a young American missionary named Allen Dutton. Allen befriended Daniel and taught him about Jesus Christ. Daniel and his wife soon became Christians and devoted disciples.

But though Daniel had been forgiven so much, he still found it impossible to forgive his brother. The wound was deep. The pot of revenge still simmered. He didn't see his brother for two years. Daniel couldn't bring himself to look into the face of the one who had betrayed him. And his brother liked his own face too much to let Daniel see it.

But an encounter was inevitable. Both knew they would eventually run into each other. And neither knew what would happen then.

The encounter occurred one day on a busy avenue. Let Daniel tell you in his own words what happened:

> I saw him, but he didn't see me. I felt my fists clench and my face get hot. My initial impulse was to grab him around the throat and choke the life out of him.
>
> But as I looked into his face, my anger began to melt. For as I saw him, I saw the image of my father. I saw my father's eyes. I saw my father's look. I saw my father's expression. And as I saw my father in his face, my enemy once again became my brother.

———

Daniel walked toward him. The brother stopped, turned, and started to run, but he was too slow. Daniel reached out and grabbed his shoulder. The brother winced, expecting the worst. But rather than have his throat squeezed by Daniel's hands, he found himself hugged by Daniel's big arms. And the two brothers stood in the middle of the river of people and wept.

Daniel's words are worth repeating: "When I saw the image of my father in his face, my enemy became my brother."

Seeing the father's image in the face of the enemy. Try that. The next time you see or think of the one who broke your heart, look twice. As you look at his face, look also for his face—the face of the One who forgave you. Look into the eyes of the King who wept when you pleaded for mercy. Look into the face of the Father who gave you grace when no one else gave you a chance. Find the face of the God who forgives in the face of your enemy. And then, because God has forgiven you more than you'll ever be called on to forgive in another, set your enemy—and yourself—free.

And allow the hole in your heart to heal.

CHAPTER TWELVE

THE STATE OF
THE HEART

Blessed are the pure in heart . . .

I CAN STILL REMEMBER THE FIRST TIME I SAW ONE. I HAD GONE
to work with my dad—a big thrill for a ten-year-old whose father
worked in the oil fields. I sat in the cab of the pickup as tall as I
could, stretching to see the endless West Texas plain. The countryside was flat and predictable, boasting nothing taller than pumpjacks
and windmills. Maybe that is why the thing seemed so colossal. It
stood out on the horizon like a science-fiction city.

"What's that?"

"It's a refinery," Dad answered.

A jungle of pipes and tanks and tubes and generators—heaters, pumps, pipes, filters, valves, hoses, conduits, switches, circuits. It looked like a giant Tinkertoy set.

The function of that maze of machinery is defined by its name: It refines. Gasoline, oil, chemicals—the refinery takes whatever comes in and purifies it so that it's ready to go out.

The refinery does for petroleum and other products what your "heart" should do for you. It takes out the bad and utilizes the good.

We tend to think of the heart as the seat of emotion. We speak of "heartthrobs," "heartaches," and "broken hearts."

But when Jesus said, "Blessed are the pure in heart," he was speaking in a different context. To Jesus' listeners, the heart was the totality of the inner person—the control tower, the cockpit. The heart was thought of as the seat of the character—the origin of desires, affections, perceptions, thoughts, reasoning, imagination, conscience, intentions, purpose, will, and faith.

Thus a proverb admonished, "Above all else, guard your heart, for it is the wellspring of life."[1]

To the Hebrew mind, the heart is a freeway cloverleaf where all emotions and prejudices and wisdom converge. It is a switch house that receives freight cars loaded with moods, ideas, emotions, and convictions and puts them on the right track.

And just as a low-grade oil or alloyed gasoline would cause you to question the performance of a refinery, evil acts and impure thoughts cause us to question the condition of our hearts.

But the things that come out of the mouth come from the heart, and these make a man "unclean." For out of the heart come evil thoughts, murder, adultery, sexual immorality, theft, false testimony, slander.[2]

The good man brings good things out of the good stored up in his heart, and the evil man brings evil things out of the evil stored up in his heart. For out of the overflow of his heart his mouth speaks.[3]

These verses hammer home the same truth: The heart is the center of the spiritual life. If the fruit of a tree is bad, you don't try to fix the fruit; you treat the roots. And if a person's actions are evil, it's not enough to change habits; you have to go deeper. You have to go to the heart of the problem, which is the problem of the heart.

That is why the state of the heart is so critical. What's the state of yours?

When someone barks at you, do you bark back or bite your tongue? That depends on the state of your heart.

When your schedule is too tight or your to-do list too long, do you lose your cool or keep it? That depends on the state of your heart.

When you are offered a morsel of gossip marinated in slander, do you turn it down or pass it on? That depends on the state of your heart.

Do you see the bag lady on the street as a burden on society or as an opportunity for God? That, too, depends on the state of your heart.

The state of your heart dictates whether you harbor a grudge or give grace, seek self-pity or seek Christ, drink human misery or taste God's mercy.

No wonder, then, the wise man begs, "Above all else, guard your heart."

David's prayer should be ours: "Create in me a pure heart, O God."[4]

And Jesus' statement rings true: "Blessed are the pure in heart, for they shall see God."

Note the order of this beatitude: *first*, purify the heart, *then you* will see God. Clean the refinery, and the result will be a pure product.

We usually reverse the order. We try to change the inside by altering the outside. Let me give you an example.

When my family lived in Rio de Janeiro, I owned a ham radio. I kept it in the utility room on top of the freezer. When we traveled, I always unplugged the radio and disconnected the antenna.

Once, when we were leaving for a week-long trip, I remembered I hadn't unplugged the radio. I ran back in the house, pulled the plug, and dashed out again.

But I pulled the wrong plug. I unplugged the freezer. It was summertime, and summer in Rio redefines the word *hot*. Our apartment was on the top of a fourteen-floor apartment building, which adds another degree of intensity to the word *hot*. For seven days, then, a freezer full of food sat in a sweltering apartment with the power off. (Why are you groaning?)

When we came home, Denalyn decided to get some meat out of the freezer. As she opened the freezer door—well, I won't go into details as to what she saw, but I will say it was a moving experience.

Guess who got fingered as the one who had unplugged the freezer—and who therefore would be responsible for cleaning it? You got it. So I got to work.

What is the best way to clean out a rotten interior? I knew exactly what to do. I got a rag and a bucket of soapy water and began cleaning the outside of the appliance. I was sure the odor would disappear with a good shine, so I polished and buffed and wiped. When I was through, the freezer could have passed a Marine boot-camp inspection. It was sparkling.

But when I opened the door, that freezer was revolting.

(Are you wondering, "Now what kind of fool would do that?" Read on and you'll see.)

No problem, I thought. I knew what to do. This freezer needs some friends. I'd stink, too, if I had the social life of a machine in a utility room. So, I threw a party. I invited all the appliances from the neighborhood kitchens. It was hard work, but we filled our apartment with refrigerators, stoves, microwaves, and washing machines. It was a great party. A couple of toasters recognized each other from the appliance store. Everyone played pin the plug on the socket and had a few laughs about limited warranties. The blenders were the hit, though; they really mixed well.

I was sure the social interaction would cure the inside of my freezer, but I was wrong. I opened it up, and the stink was even worse!

Now what?

I had an idea. If a polish job wouldn't do it and a social life didn't help, I'd give the freezer some status!

I bought a Mercedes sticker and stuck it on the door. I painted a paisley tie down the front. I put a "Save the Whales" bumper sticker on the rear and installed a cellular phone on the side. That freezer was classy. It was stylish. It was . . . cool. I splashed it with cologne and gave it a credit card for clout.

Then I backed away and admired the high-class freezer. "You just might make the cover of *Popular Mechanics*," I told it. It blushed. Then I opened the door, expecting to see a clean inside, but what I saw was putrid—a stinky and repulsive interior.

I could think of only one other option. My freezer needed some high-voltage pleasure! I immediately bought it some copies of *Playfridge* magazine—the publication that displays freezers with their doors open. I rented some films about foxy appliances. (My favorite was *The Big Chill*.) I even tried to get my freezer a date with the Westinghouse next door, but she gave him the cold shoulder.

After a few days of supercharged, after-hours entertainment, I opened the door. And I nearly got sick.

I know what you're thinking. The only thing worse than Max's humor is his common sense. Who would concentrate on the outside when the problem is on the inside?

Do you really want to know?

A homemaker battles with depression. What is the solution suggested by some well-meaning friend? Buy a new dress.

A husband is involved in an affair that brings him as much guilt as it does adventure. The solution? Change peer groups. Hang out with people who don't make you feel guilty!

A young professional is plagued with loneliness. His obsession with success has left him with no friends. His boss gives him an idea: Change your style. Get a new haircut. Flash some cash.

Case after case of treating the outside while ignoring the

inside—polishing the case while ignoring the interior. And what is the result?

The homemaker gets a new dress, and the depression disappears . . . for a day, maybe. Then the shadow returns.

The husband finds a bunch of buddies who sanction his adultery. The result? Peace . . . until the crowd is gone. Then the guilt is back.

The young professional gets a new look and the people notice . . . until the styles change. Then he has to scurry out and buy more stuff so he won't appear outdated.

The exterior polished; the interior corroding. The outside altered; the inside faltering. One thing is clear: Cosmetic changes are only skin deep.

By now you could write the message of the beatitude. It's a clear one: You change your life by changing your heart.

❧

How do you change your heart? Jesus gave the plan on the mountain. Back away from the beatitudes once more and view them in sequence.

The first step is an admission of poverty: "Blessed are the poor in spirit. . . ." God's gladness is not received by those who earn it, but by those who admit they *don't* deserve it. The joy of Sarah, Peter, and Paul came when they surrendered, when they pleaded for a lifeguard instead of a swimming lesson, when they sought a savior instead of a system.

The second step is sorrow: "Blessed are those who mourn. . . ." Joy comes to those who are sincerely sorry for their sin. We discover gladness when we leave the prison of pride and repent of our rebellion.

Sorrow is followed by meekness. The meek are those who are willing to be used by God. Amazed that God would save them, they are just as surprised that God could use them. They are a junior-high-school clarinet section playing with the Boston Pops. They don't tell the maestro how to conduct; they're just thrilled to be part of the concert.

The result of the first three steps? Hunger. Never have you seen anything like what is happening! You admit sin—you get saved. You confess weakness—you receive strength. You say you are sorry—you find forgiveness. It's a zany, unpredictable path full of pleasant encounters. For once in your life you're addicted to something positive—something that gives life instead of draining it. And you want more.

Then comes mercy. The more you receive, the more you give. You find it easier to give grace because you realize you have been given so much. What has been done to you is nothing compared to what you did to God.

For the first time in your life, you have found a permanent joy, a joy that is not dependent upon your whims and actions. It's a joy from God, a joy no one can take away from you.

A sacred delight is placed in your heart.

It is sacred because only God can grant it.

It is a delight because you would never expect it.

And though your heart isn't perfect, it isn't rotten. And though you aren't invincible, at least you're plugged in. And you can bet that he who made you knows just how to purify you—from the inside out.

CHAPTER THIRTEEN

NICE PALACE
BUT NO KING

. . . for they will see God.

ONCE, LONG AGO, THERE LIVED A KING WHO HAD MANY WIVES.
As his kingdom flourished, so had his harem. But, of all his wives,
he loved one most.

When the favorite wife died, the king grieved deeply. Devastated,
he resolved to honor her by constructing a temple that would serve
as her tomb. Her coffin was placed in the center of a large parcel of
land, and construction of the temple began around it. No expense
would be spared to make her final resting place magnificent.

But as the weeks turned into months, the king's grief was

eclipsed by his passion for the project. He no longer mourned her absence. The construction consumed him. One day, while walking from one side of the construction site to the other, his leg bumped against a wooden box. The king's son brushed the dust off his leg and ordered the worker to throw the box out.

The king didn't know he had ordered the disposal of the coffin—now forgotten—hidden beneath layers of dust and time.

The one the temple was intended to honor was forgotten, but the temple was erected anyway.

Difficult to believe? Perhaps. But eerie nonetheless.

Could someone build a temple and forget why? Could someone construct a palace, yet forget the king? Could someone sculpt a tribute and forget the hero?

You answer those questions. Answer them in a church. The next time you enter an assembly of worship, position yourself where you can see the people. Then decide.

You can tell the ones who remember the slain one. They're wide-eyed and expectant. They're children watching the unwrapping of a gift. They're servants standing still as a king passes. You don't doze in the presence of royalty. And you don't yawn while receiving a gift, especially when the giver is the King himself!

You can also tell the ones who see only the temple. Their eyes wander. Their feet shuffle. Their hands doodle, and their mouths open—not to sing, but to yawn. For no matter how hard they try to stay amazed, their eyes start to glaze over. All temples lose their luster after a while.

The temple gazers don't mean to be bored. They love the church. They can cite its programs and praise its pastors. They don't mean to grow stale. They put on hats and hose and coats and ties and come every week. But still, something is missing. The One they once planned to honor hasn't been seen in a while.

But those who have seen him can't seem to forget him. They find him, often in spite of the temple rather than because of it. They brush the dust away and stand ever impressed before his tomb— his empty tomb.

The temple builders and the Savior seekers. You'll find them both in the same church, on the same pew—at times, even in the same suit. One sees the structure and says, "What a great church." The other sees the Savior and says, "What a great Christ!"

Which do you see?

Chapter Fourteen

SEEDS OF PEACE

Blessed are the peacemakers . . .

WANT TO SEE A MIRACLE? TRY THIS.

Take a seed the size of a freckle. Put it under several inches of dirt. Give it enough water, light, and fertilizer. And get ready. A mountain will be moved. It doesn't matter that the ground is a zillion times the weight of the seed. The seed will push it back.

Every spring, dreamers around the world plant tiny hopes in overturned soil. And every spring, their hopes press against impossible odds and blossom.

Never underestimate the power of a seed.

As far as I know, James, the epistle writer, wasn't a farmer. But he knew the power of a seed sown in fertile soil.

"Those who are peacemakers will plant seeds of peace and reap a harvest of goodness."[1]

The principle for peace is the same as the principle for crops: Never underestimate the power of a seed.

The story of Heinz is a good example. Europe, 1934. Hitler's plague of anti-Semitism was infecting a continent. Some would escape it. Some would die from it. But eleven-year-old Heinz would learn from it. He would learn the power of sowing seeds of peace.

Heinz was a Jew.

The Bavarian village of Furth, where Heinz lived, was being over-run by Hitler's young thugs. Heinz's father, a schoolteacher, lost his job. Recreational activities ceased. Tension mounted on the streets.

The Jewish families clutched the traditions that held them together—the observance of the Sabbath, of Rosh Hashanah, of Yom Kippur. Old ways took on new significance. As the clouds of persecution swelled and blackened, these ancient precepts were a precious cleft in a mighty rock.

And as the streets became a battleground, such security meant survival.

Hitler youth roamed the neighborhoods looking for trouble. Young Heinz learned to keep his eyes open. When he saw a band of troublemakers, he would step to the other side of the street. Sometimes he would escape a fight—sometimes not.

One day, in 1934, a pivotal confrontation occurred. Heinz found himself face-to-face with a Hitler bully. A beating appeared inevitable. This time, however, he walked away unhurt—not because of what he did, but because of what he said. He didn't fight back; he spoke up. He convinced the troublemakers that a fight was not necessary. His words kept battle at bay.

And Heinz saw firsthand how the tongue can create peace.

He learned the skill of using words to avoid conflict. And for a young Jew in Hitler-ridden Europe, that skill had many opportunities to be honed.

Fortunately, Heinz's family escaped from Bavaria and made their way to America. Later in life, he would downplay the impact those adolescent experiences had on his development.

But one has to wonder. For after Heinz grew up, his name became synonymous with peace negotiations. His legacy became that of a bridge builder. Somewhere he had learned the power of the properly placed word of peace. And one has to wonder if his training didn't come on the streets of Bavaria.

You don't know him as Heinz. You know him by his Anglicized name, Henry. Henry Kissinger.[2]

Never underestimate the power of a seed.

How good are you at sowing seeds of peace?

You may not be called on to ward off international conflict, but you will have opportunities to do something more vital: to bring inner peace to troubled hearts.

Jesus modeled this. We don't see him settling many disputes or negotiating conflicts. But we *do* see him cultivating inward harmony through acts of love:

washing the feet of men he knew would betray him,

having lunch with a corrupt tax official,

honoring the sinful woman whom society had scorned.

He built bridges by healing hurts. He prevented conflict by touching the interior. He cultivated harmony by sowing seeds of peace in fertile hearts.

Do me a favor. Pause for a moment and think about the people who make up your world. Take a stroll through the gallery of faces that are significant to you. Mentally flip through the scrapbook of snapshots featuring those you deal with often.

Can you see their faces? Your spouse. Your best friend. Your golf buddies. Your friends at PTA. Your kids. Your aunt across the country. Your neighbor across the street. The receptionist at work. The new secretary in the next office.

Freeze-frame those mental images for a moment while I tell you how some of them are feeling.

I went to our family doctor not long ago. I went for my first check-up since the one required for high school football seventeen years ago.

Since I was way overdue, I ordered the works. One nurse put me on a table and stuck little cold suction cups to my chest. Another nurse wrapped a heavy band around my arm and squeezed a black bulb until my arm tingled. Then they pricked my finger (which always hurts) and told me to fill up a cup (which is always awkward). Then, with all the preliminaries done, they put me in a room and told me to take off my shirt and wait on the doctor.

There is something about being poked, pushed, measured, and drained that makes you feel like a head of lettuce in the produce department. I sat on a tiny stool and stared at the wall.

May I tell you something you know, but may have forgotten? Somebody in your world feels like I felt in that office. The daily push and shove of the world has a way of leaving us worked over and worn out. Someone in your gallery of people is sitting on a cold aluminum stool of insecurity, clutching the backside of a hospital gown for fear of exposing what little pride he or she has left. And that person desperately needs a word of peace.

Someone needs you to do for them what Dr. Jim did for me.

Jim is a small-town doctor in a big city. He still remembers names and keeps pictures of babies he delivered on his office bulletin board. And though you know he's busy, he makes you feel you are his only patient.

After a bit of small talk and a few questions about my medical history, he put down my file and said, "Let me take off my doctor hat for a minute and talk to you as a friend."

The chat lasted maybe five minutes. He asked me about my family. He asked me about my workload. He asked me about my stress. He told me he thought I was doing a good job at the church and that he loved to read my books.

Nothing profound, nothing probing. He went no deeper than I allowed. But I had the feeling he would have gone to the bottom of the pit with me had I needed him to.

After those few minutes, Dr. Jim went about his task of tapping my knee with his rubber hammer, staring down my throat, looking in my ear, and listening to my chest. When he was all done, as I was buttoning up my shirt, he took his doctor hat off again and reminded me not to carry the world on my shoulders. "And be sure to love your wife and hug those kids, because when it all boils down to it, you're not much without them."

"Thanks, Jim," I said.

And he walked out as quickly as he'd come in—a seed sower in a physician's smock.

Want to see a miracle? Plant a word of love heartdeep in a person's life. Nurture it with a smile and a prayer, and watch what happens.

An employee gets a compliment. A wife receives a bouquet of flowers. A cake is baked and carried next door. A widow is hugged. A gas-station attendant is honored. A preacher is praised.

Sowing seeds of peace is like sowing beans. You don't know why it works; you just know it does. Seeds are planted, and topsoils of hurt are shoved away.

Don't forget the principle. Never underestimate the power of a seed.

God didn't. When his kingdom was ravaged and his people had forgotten his name, he planted his seed.

When the soil of the human heart had grown crusty, he planted his seed. When religion had become a ritual and the temple a trading post, he planted his seed.

Want to see a miracle? Watch him as he places the seed of his own self in the fertile womb of a Jewish girl.

Up it grew, "like a tender green shoot, sprouting from a root in dry and sterile ground."[3] The seed spent a lifetime pushing back the stones that tried to keep it underground. The seed made a ministry out of shoving away the rocks that cluttered his Father's soil.

The stones of legalism that burdened backs.

The stones of oppression that broke bones.

The stones of prejudice that fenced out the needy.

But it was the final stone that proved to be the supreme test of the seed. The stone of death—rolled by humans and sealed by Satan in front of the tomb. For a moment it appeared the seed would be stuck in the earth. For a moment, it looked like this rock was too big to be budged.

But then, somewhere in the heart of the earth, the seed of God stirred, shoved, and sprouted. The ground trembled, and the rock of the tomb tumbled. And the flower of Easter blossomed.

Never underestimate the power of a seed.

CHAPTER FIFTEEN

THE GREASY POLE
OF POWER

. . . for they will be called sons of God.

THE PUSH FOR POWER HAS COME TO SHOVE.

You know the power lingo. You know the power plays. You have a power wardrobe.

You think you have everything you need for power? Think twice and come to dinner. Now there are power table manners.

"Manners will take you where your money can't," states the "Queen of Courtesy," Marjabelle Stewart. This crusader for couth has developed a seminar to help you eat your way to the top. For six thousand dollars you can sit in on a seminar and learn the manners that have clout.

Here are a few examples of what Stewart calls "power failures":

- Never tuck your napkin into your collar.
- Never leave a lipstick mark on the rim of a glass.
- Never mash or stir your food.
- Never haggle over the bill.
- Never, ever, hand your plate to the waiter.
- Never read the menu like a Bible. You aren't there to eat, but to do business.
- Never stoop down to retrieve dropped silver.[1]

In fact, the primary rule of thumb in the quest for power is never to stoop down for anything.

Never stoop to appear weak. Never stoop to admit mistakes. Never stoop to help someone who could never help you. Never stoop to any level that might loosen your grip on your rung of the ladder.

Add "power etiquette" to "name dropping," "card flashing," and "title touting." Put it on the long list of games we play to make a name for ourselves.

"Power moves" are simply "King of the Mountain" on an adult level.

Remember playing that game as a kid? The object of the game is to get high on the heap and stay there. You push, claw, and climb until you get to the top. And once you get there, you fight to hold your position. Don't even think about sitting down. Forget enjoying the view. Slack up for even a minute, and you'll be slapped down to the bottom of the hill. And then you'll have to start all over again.

As grown-ups we still play "King of the Mountain," but now

the stakes are higher. Harrison Ford in the movie *Working Girl* put it this way:

> One lost deal is all it takes to get canned these days. The line buttons on my phone all have an inch of little pieces of tape piled on—the names of new guys over the names of old guys— good men who aren't at the other end of the line anymore all because of one lost deal. I don't want to get buried under a little piece of tape.

The push for power has come to shove. And most of us are either pushing or being pushed.

I might point out the difference between a passion for excellence and a passion for power. The desire for excellence is a gift of God, much needed in society. It is characterized by respect for quality and a yearning to use God's gifts in a way that pleases him. Recall the words of Antonio Stradivari, the seventeenth-century violin maker whose name in its Latin form, Stradivarius, has become synonymous with excellence:

> When any master holds 'twixt chin and hand a violin of mine, he will be glad that Stradivari lived, made violins and made them of the best. . . . If my hand slacked I should rob God— since he is the fullest good. . . . But he could not make Antonio Stradivari's violins without Antonio.[2]

He was right. God could not make Stradivarius violins without Antonio Stradivari. Certain gifts were given to that craftsman that no other violin maker possessed.

In the same vein, there are certain things you can do that no one else can. Perhaps it is parenting, or constructing houses, or encouraging the discouraged. There are things that *only you* can do, and you are alive to do them. In the great orchestra we call life, you have an instrument and a song, and you owe it to God to play them both sublimely.

But there is a canyon of difference between doing your best to glorify God and doing whatever it takes to glorify yourself. The quest for excellence is a mark of maturity. The quest for power is childish.

It might interest you to know that the first power play happened not on Wall Street nor on a battlefield, but in a garden. The first promise of prestige was whispered with a hiss, a wink, and a snakish grin by a fallen angel.

Standing in the shadow of the tree of the knowledge of good and evil, Satan knew what to offer Eve to convince her to eat the apple. It wasn't pleasure. It wasn't health. It wasn't prosperity. It was . . . well, you read his words and look for his lure:

"God knows that when you eat of it your eyes will be opened, and you will be like God, knowing good and evil."[3]

The words found a soft spot.

"You will be like God. . . ."

Eve stroked her chin as she replayed the promise.

"You will be like God. . . ."

The snake pulled back the curtain to the throne room and invited Eve to take a seat. Put on the crown. Pick up the scepter.

Put on the cape. See how it feels to have power. See how it feels to have a name. See how it feels to be in control!

Eve swallowed the hook. The temptation to be *like* God eclipsed her view of God, and the crunch of an apple echoed in the kingdom. You know the rest of the story.

Now, perhaps your flirtations with power haven't been so blatant. No doubt, you were amused at the thought of spending six grand on a table manners seminar. No doubt you've shaken your head in amazement at the buy-outs staged by the barons of Wall Street. No doubt you've been chagrined by the murders ordered by drug lords and kingpins. That type of power play has no attraction for you. If the snake were to woo you with promises of status, you'd send him back to the pit, right?

Or would you? "King of the Mountain" comes in many forms.

It's the boss who won't compliment her employees. After all, workers need to be kept in their place.

It's the husband who refuses to be kind to his wife. He knows if he does he will lose his most powerful weapon—her fear of his rejection.

It's the employee who places personal ambition over personal integrity.

It's the wife who withholds sex both to punish and persuade.

It might be the taking of someone's life, or it might be the taking of someone's turn. It might be manipulation with a pistol, or it might be manipulation with a pout. It might be the takeover of a nation by a politician, or the takeover of a church by a preacher.

But they are all spelled the same: P-O-W-E-R.

All have the same goal: "I will get what I want at your expense."

All have the same game plan: push, shove, take, and lie.

All have listened to the same snake, the same lying Lucifer who whispers into the ears of anyone who will listen, "You will be like God."

And all have the same end: futility. Please note carefully what I am about to say. Absolute power is unreachable. The pole to the top is greasy, and the ladder rungs are made of cardboard. When you stand at the top—if there is a top—the only way to go is down. And the descent is often painful.

Ask Muhammad Ali.

You know Ali, the unprecedented three-time world heavy-weight boxing champion. His face has appeared on the cover of *Sports Illustrated* more times than any other athlete. When he was "floating like a butterfly and stinging like a bee," he was king of his profession. An entourage of reporters, trainers, and support staff tailed this comet as he raced around the world.

But that was yesterday. Where is Muhammad Ali today? Sportswriter Gary Smith went to find out.

Ali escorted Smith to a barn next to his farmhouse. On the floor, leaning against the walls, were mementos of Ali in his prime. Photos and portraits of the champ punching and dancing. Sculpted body. Fist punching the air. Championship belt held high in triumph. "The thrilla in Manila."

But on the pictures were white streaks—bird droppings. Ali looked into the rafters at the pigeons who had made his gym their home. And then he did something significant. Perhaps it was a gesture of closure. Maybe it was a statement of despair. Whatever the reason, he walked over to the row of pictures and turned them, one by one, toward the wall. He then walked to the door, stared at the countryside, and mumbled something so low that Smith had to ask him to repeat it. Ali did.

"I had the world," he said, "and it wasn't nothin'. Look now."[4]

The pole of power is greasy.

The Roman emperor Charlemagne knew that. An interesting story surrounds the burial of this famous king. Legend has it that he asked to be entombed sitting upright in his throne. He asked that his crown be placed on his head and his scepter in his hand. He requested that the royal cape be draped around his shoulders and an open book be placed in his lap.

That was AD 814. Nearly two hundred years later, Emperor Othello determined to see if the burial request had been carried out. He allegedly sent a team of men to open the tomb and make a report. They found the body just as Charlemagne had requested. Only now, nearly two centuries later, the scene was gruesome. The crown was tilted, the mantle moth-eaten, the body disfigured. But open on the skeletal thighs was the book Charlemagne had requested—the Bible. One bony finger pointed to Matthew 16:26: "What good will it be for a man if he gains the whole world, yet forfeits his soul?"[5]

You can answer that one.

As these thoughts on power were beginning to take shape, I found myself at a banquet.

Now, on my list of favorite things to do on a free evening, attending a banquet is pretty close to the bottom. The thought conjures up images of cold food, hot rooms, poor sound systems, long-winded speakers, and gravy spots on my tie. Forgive my social maladjustment, but I'll take a good movie or baseball game anytime.

This particular banquet was doing little to change my opinion.

It was an awards ceremony that had been overbooked and had begun late. The master of ceremonies was having a hard time keeping everyone's attention. He competed against a squad of waiters that darted in and dashed out every thirteen seconds. The awards were presented with meticulous detail. They were received with explicit—and verbose—gratitude. I began looking at my watch and munching on ice cubes.

That's when the king was introduced.

"A king?" I looked around, thinking I would see a cape and a crown. I didn't. I did see a nicely dressed young man escorted to the platform.

"So that is what a king looks like," I thought. Others must have been just as intrigued. The place was silent.

King Goodwill was his name. He is a seventh-generation king of the Zulu tribe in Africa. Impressive title. But more significant was the fact that King Goodwill himself had a King. Goodwill was a believer. He had embraced Christ as his Lord and was encouraging his nation to do the same.

Though King Goodwill's entire speech was noteworthy, it was his first phrase that I copied in my date book: "I am a king, but I greet you as my brothers."

A king who considers me his brother. A ruler who welcomes me into his family. Royalty freely granted.

His words reminded me of another King who did the same.

"Blessed are the peacemakers, for they will be called sons of God."

"Be a power broker," the snake lied, "and you will be like God."

"Be a peacemaker," the King promised, "and you will be a son of God."

Which would you prefer? To be king of the mountain for a day? Or to be a child of God for eternity?

There is a side benefit to sonship. If you are a child of God, then what does the world have to offer? Can you have any greater title than the one you have?

Answer this: A thousand years from now, will it matter what title the world gave you? No, but it will make a literal hell of a difference whose child you are.

One final note about that banquet. After it was over, I stuck around, hoping to meet the king. At first I couldn't find him. Then I came across him and his wife and assistants in a side hall. Guess what they were doing? Laughing! Somebody must have told a whopper of a joke, because this group could barely stand up.

A king in stitches. What a delight.

A belly laugh is not what I would call a power play. It could better be described as a good time. I guess when you're a king, you don't have to worry about being proper for the sake of status; you already have all you need.

That goes for children of the King, too.

Next time I eat, I think I'll tuck my napkin in my collar.

CHAPTER SIXTEEN

THE DUNGEON
OF DOUBT

---

*Blessed are those who are persecuted
because of righteousness . . .*

HE WAS A CHILD OF THE DESERT. LEATHERY FACE. TANNED skin. Clothing of animal skins. What he owned fit in a pouch. His walls were the mountains and his ceiling the stars.

But not anymore. His frontier is walled out, his horizon hidden. The stars are memories. The fresh air is all but forgotten. And the stench of the dungeon relentlessly reminds the child of the desert that he is now a captive of the king.[1]

In anyone's book, John the Baptist deserves better treatment

---

than this. After all, isn't he the forerunner of the Christ? Isn't he a relative of the Messiah? At the very least, isn't his the courageous voice of repentance?

But most recently that voice, instead of opening the door of renewal, has opened the door to his own prison cell.

John's problems began when he called a king on the carpet.

On a trip to Rome, King Herod succumbed to the enticements of his brother's wife, Herodias. Deciding Herodias was better off married to him, Herod divorced his wife and brought his sister-in-law home.

The gossip columnists were fascinated, but John the Baptist was infuriated. He pounced on Herod like a desert scorpion, denouncing the marriage for what it was—adultery.

Herod might have let him get away with it. But not Herodias. This steamy seductress wasn't about to have her social climbing exposed. She told Herod to have John pulled off the speaking circuit and thrown into the dungeon. Herod hemmed and hawed until she whispered and wooed. Then Herod gave in.

But that wasn't enough for this mistress. She had her daughter strut before the king and his generals at a stag party. Herod, who was as easily duped as he was aroused, promised to do anything for the pretty young thing in the G-string.

"Anything?"

"You name it," he drooled.

She conferred with her mother, who was waiting in the wings, then returned with her request.

"I want John the Baptist."

"You want a date with the prophet?"

"I want his head," replied the dancer. And then, reassured by a nod from her mother, she added, "On a silver platter, if you don't mind."

Herod looked at the faces around him. He knew it wasn't fair, but he also knew everyone was looking at him. And he *had* promised "anything." Though he personally had nothing against the country preacher, he valued the opinion polls much more than he valued John's life. After all, what's more important—to save face or to save the neck of an eccentric prophet?

The story reeks with inequity.

John dies because Herod lusts.

The good is murdered while the bad smirk.

A man of God is killed while a man of passion is winking at his niece.

Is this how God rewards his anointed? Is this how he honors his faithful? Is this how God crowns his chosen? With a dark dungeon and a shiny blade?

The inconsistency was more than John could take. Even before Herod reached his verdict, John was asking his questions. His concerns were outnumbered only by the number of times he paced his cell asking them. When he had a chance to get a message to Jesus, his inquiry was one of despair:

"When John heard in prison what Christ was doing, he sent his disciples to ask him, 'Are you the one who was to come, or should we expect someone else?'"[2]

Note what motivated John's question. It was not just the dungeon or even death. It was the problem of unmet expectations—the fact that John was in deep trouble and Jesus was conducting business as usual.

Is this what messiahs do when trouble comes? Is this what God does when his followers are in a bind?

Jesus' silence was enough to chisel a leak into the dam of John's belief. "Are you the one? Or have I been following the wrong Lord?"

Had the Bible been written by a public relations agency, they would have eliminated that verse. It's not good PR strategy to admit that one of the cabinet members has doubts about the president. You don't let stories like that get out if you are trying to present a unified front.

But the Scriptures weren't written by personality agents; they were inspired by an eternal God who knew that every disciple from then on would spend time in the dungeon of doubt.

Though the circumstances have changed, the questions haven't.

They are asked anytime the faithful suffer the consequences of the faithless. Anytime a person takes a step in the right direction, only to have her feet knocked out from under her, anytime a person does a good deed but suffers evil results, anytime a person takes a stand, only to end up flat on his face . . . the questions fall like rain:

"If God is so good, why do I hurt so bad?"

"If God is really there, why am I here?"

"What did I do to deserve this?"

"Did God slip up this time?"

"Why are the righteous persecuted?"

In his book *Disappointment with God*, Philip Yancey quotes a letter that articulates the problem of unmet expectations in all its excruciating reality. Meg Woodson lost two children to cystic fibrosis, and her daughter's death at age twenty-three was particularly traumatic. The following words speak of her pain and doubt as she struggled to cope with what happened:

> I was sitting beside her bed a few days before her death when suddenly she began screaming. I will never forget those shrill, piercing, primal screams. . . . It's against this background of human beings falling apart . . . that God, who could have helped, looked down on a young woman devoted to Him, quite willing to die for Him to give Him glory, and decided to sit on His hands and let her death top the horror charts for cystic fibrosis deaths.[3]

Does God sometimes sit on his hands? Does God sometimes choose to do nothing? Does God sometimes opt for silence even when I'm screaming my loudest?

Some time ago, I took my family to the bicycle store to purchase a bike for five-year-old Jenna. She picked out a shiny "Starlett" with a banana seat and training wheels. And Andrea, age three, decided she wanted one as well.

I explained to Andrea that she was too young. I told her she was still having trouble with a tricycle and was too small for a two-wheeler. No luck; she still wanted a bike. I explained to her that when she was a bit older, she would get a bike, too. She just stared at me. I tried to tell her that a big bike would bring her more pain than pleasure, more scrapes than thrills. She turned her head and said nothing.

Finally I sighed and said this time her daddy knew best. Her response? She screamed it loud enough for everyone in the store to hear:

"Then I want a *new* daddy!"

Though the words were from a child's mouth, they carried an adult's sentiments.

Disappointment demands a change in command. When we don't agree with the One who calls the shots, our reaction is often the same as Andrea's—the same as John's. "Is he the right one for this job?" Or, as John put it, "Are you the one? Should we look for another?"

Andrea, with her three-year-old reasoning powers, couldn't believe that a new bike would be anything less than ideal for her. From her vantage point, it would be the source of eternal bliss. And from her vantage point, the one who could grant that bliss was "sitting on his hands."

John couldn't believe that anything less than his release would be for the best interest of all involved. In his opinion, it was time to exercise some justice and get some action. But the One who had the power was "sitting on his hands."

I can't believe that God would sit in silence while a missionary is kicked out of a foreign country or a Christian loses a promotion because of his beliefs or a faithful wife is abused by an unbelieving husband. These are just three of many items that have made their way onto my prayer list—all prayers that seem to have gone unanswered.

Rule of thumb: Clouds of doubt are created when the warm, moist air of our expectations meets the cold air of God's silence.

If you've heard the silence of God, if you've been left standing in the dungeon of doubt, then don't put this book down until you read the next chapter. You may learn, as John did, that the problem is not as much in God's silence as it is in your ability to hear.

CHAPTER SEVENTEEN

THE KINGDOM
WORTH DYING FOR

. . . for theirs is the kingdom of heaven.

GO BACK AND REPORT TO JOHN WHAT YOU HEAR AND SEE: THE blind receive sight, the lame walk, those who have leprosy are cured, the deaf hear, the dead are raised, and the good news is preached to the poor."[1]

This was Jesus' answer to John's agonized query from the dungeon of doubt: "Are you the one who was to come, or should we expect someone else?"[2]

But before you study what Jesus said, note a couple of things he didn't say.

First, he didn't get angry. He didn't throw up his hands in disgust. He didn't scream, "What in the world do I have to do for John? I've already become flesh! I've already been sinless for three decades. I let him baptize me. What else does he want? Go and tell that ungrateful locust eater I am shocked at his disbelief."

He could have done that. (I would have done that.)

But Jesus didn't. Underline that fact: *God has never turned away the questions of a sincere searcher.* Not Job's nor Abraham's nor Moses' nor John's nor Thomas's nor Max's nor yours.

But note also that Jesus didn't save John. The One who had walked on water could have easily walked on Herod's head, but he didn't. The One who cast out the demons had the power to nuke the king's castle, but he didn't. No battle plan. No SWAT teams. No flashing swords. Just a message—a kingdom message.

"Tell John that everything is going as planned. The kingdom is being inaugurated."

Jesus' words are much more than a statement from Isaiah.[3] They are the description of a heavenly kingdom being established.

A unique kingdom. An invisible kingdom. A kingdom with three distinct traits.

First of all, it is a kingdom where the rejected are received.

"The blind receive sight, the lame walk, those who have leprosy are cured, the deaf hear. . . ."

None were more shunned by their culture than the blind, the lame, the lepers, and the deaf. They had no place. No name. No value. Canker sores on the culture. Excess baggage on the side of the road. But those whom the people called trash, Jesus called treasures.

In my closet hangs a sweater that I seldom wear. It is too small. The sleeves are too short, the shoulders too tight. Some of the buttons are missing, and the thread is frazzled. I should throw that sweater away. I have no use for it. I'll never wear it again. Logic says I should clear out the space and get rid of the sweater.

That's what *logic* says.

But *love* won't let me.

Something unique about that sweater makes me keep it. What is unusual about it? For one thing, it has no label. Nowhere on the garment will you find a tag that reads, "Made in Taiwan," or "Wash in Cold Water." It has no tag because it wasn't made in a factory. It has no label because it wasn't produced on an assembly line. It isn't the product of a nameless employee earning a living. It's the creation of a devoted mother expressing her love.

That sweater is unique. One of a kind. It can't be replaced. Each strand was chosen with care. Each thread was selected with affection.

And though the sweater has lost all of its use, it has lost none of its value. It is valuable not because of its function, but because of its maker.

That must have been what the psalmist had in mind when he wrote, "You knit me together in my mother's womb."[4]

Think on those words. You were knitted together. You aren't an accident. You weren't mass-produced. You aren't an assembly-line product. You were deliberately planned, specifically gifted, and lovingly positioned on this earth by the Master Craftsman.

"For we are God's workmanship, created in Christ Jesus to do good works, which God prepared in advance for us to do."[5]

———

In a society that has little room for second fiddles, that's good news. In a culture where the door of opportunity opens only once and then slams shut, that is a revelation. In a system that ranks the value of a human by the figures of his salary or the shape of her legs . . . let me tell you something: Jesus' plan is a reason for joy!

Jesus told John that a new kingdom was coming—a kingdom where people have value not because of what they do, but because of *whose* they are.

⌒

The second characteristic of the kingdom is as potent as the first: "The dead have life." The grave has no power.

The year 1899 marked the deaths of two well-known men—Dwight L. Moody, the acclaimed evangelist, and Robert Ingersoll, the famous lawyer, orator, and political leader.

The two men had many similarities. Both were raised in Christian homes. Both were skilled orators. Both traveled extensively and were widely respected. Both drew immense crowds when they spoke and attracted loyal followings. But there was one striking difference between them—their view of God.

Ingersoll was an agnostic and a follower of naturalism; he had no belief in the eternal, but stressed the importance of living only in the here and now. Ingersoll made light of the Bible, stating that "free thought will give us truth." To him the Bible was "a fable, an obscenity, a humbug, a sham and a lie."[6] He was a bold spokesman against the Christian faith. He claimed that a Christian "creed [was] the ignorant past bullying the enlightened present."[7]

Ingersoll's contemporary, Dwight L. Moody, had different convictions. He dedicated his life to presenting a resurrected King to a dying people. He embraced the Bible as the hope for humanity and the cross as the turning point of history. He left behind a legacy of written and spoken words, institutions of education, churches, and changed lives.

Two men. Both powerful speakers and influential leaders. One rejected God; the other embraced him. The impact of their decisions is seen most clearly in the way they died. Read how one biographer parallels the two deaths.

Ingersoll died suddenly. The news of his death stunned his family. His body was kept at home for several days because his wife was reluctant to part with it. It was eventually removed for the sake of the family's health.

Ingersoll's remains were cremated, and the public response to his passing was altogether dismal. For a man who put all his hopes on this world, death was tragic and came without the consolation of hope.

Moody's legacy was different. On December 22, 1899, Moody awoke to his last winter dawn. Having grown increasingly weak during the night, he began to speak in slow measured words. "Earth recedes, heaven opens before me!" Son Will, who was nearby, hurried across the room to his father's side.

"Father, you are dreaming," he said.

"No. This is no dream, Will," Moody said. "It is beautiful. It is like a trance. If this is death, it is sweet. God is calling me, and I must go. Don't call me back."

At that point, the family gathered around, and moments later the great evangelist died. It was his coronation day—a day he had looked forward to for many years. He was with his Lord.

The funeral service of Dwight L. Moody reflected that

same confidence. There was no despair. Loved ones gathered to sing praise to God at a triumphant home-going service. Many remembered the words the evangelist had spoken earlier that year in New York City: "Someday you will read in the papers that Moody is dead. Don't you believe a word of it. At that moment I shall be more alive than I am now. . . . I was born of the flesh in 1837, I was born of the Spirit in 1855. That which is born of the flesh may die. That which is born of the Spirit shall live forever."[8]

Jesus looked into the eyes of John's followers and gave them this message. "Report to John . . . the dead are raised." Jesus wasn't oblivious to John's imprisonment. He wasn't blind to John's captivity. But he was dealing with a greater dungeon than Herod's; he was dealing with the dungeon of death.

But Jesus wasn't through. He passed on one other message to clear the cloud of doubt out of John's heart: "The good news is preached to the poor."

Some months ago I was late to catch a plane out of the San Antonio airport. I wasn't terribly late, but I was late enough to be bumped and have my seat given to a stand-by passenger.

When the ticket agent told me that I would have to miss the flight, I put to work my best persuasive powers.

"But the flight hasn't left yet."

"Yes, but you got here too late."

"I got here before the plane left; is that too late?"

"The regulation says you must arrive ten minutes before the flight is scheduled to depart. That was two minutes ago."

"But, ma'am," I pleaded, "I've got to be in Houston by this evening."

She was patient but firm. "I'm sorry, sir, but the rules say passengers must be at the gate ten minutes before scheduled departure time."

"I know what the rules say," I explained. "But I'm not asking for justice; I'm asking for mercy."

She didn't give it to me.

But God does. Even though by the "book" I'm guilty, by God's love I get another chance. Even though by the law I'm indicted, by mercy I'm given a fresh start.

"For it is by grace you have been saved . . . not by works, so that no one can boast."[9]

No other world religion offers such a message. All others demand the right performance, the right sacrifice, the right chant, the right ritual, the right séance or experience. Theirs is a kingdom of trade-offs and barterdom. You do this, and God will give you that.

The result? Either arrogance or fear. Arrogance if you think you've achieved it, fear if you think you haven't.

Christ's kingdom is just the opposite. It is a kingdom for the poor. A kingdom where membership is *granted*, not *purchased*. You are placed into God's kingdom. You are "adopted." And this occurs not when you do enough, but when you admit you *can't* do enough. You don't earn it; you simply accept it. As a result, you serve, not out of arrogance or fear, but out of gratitude.

I recently read a story of a woman who for years was married to a harsh husband. Each day he would leave her a list of chores to complete before he returned at the end of the day. "Clean the yard. Stack the firewood. Wash the windows. . . ."

If she didn't complete the tasks, she would be greeted with his explosive anger. But even if she did complete the list, he was never satisfied; he would always find inadequacies in her work.

After several years, the husband passed away. Some time later she remarried, this time to a man who lavished her with tenderness and adoration.

One day, while going through a box of old papers, the wife discovered one of her first husband's lists. And as she read the sheet, a realization caused a tear of joy to splash on the paper.

"I'm still doing all these things, and no one has to tell me. I do it because I love him."

That is the unique characteristic of the new kingdom. Its subjects don't work in order to go to heaven; they work *because* they are going to heaven. Arrogance and fear are replaced with gratitude and joy.

⤒

That's the kingdom Jesus proclaimed: a kingdom of acceptance, eternal life, and forgiveness.

We don't know how John received Jesus' message, but we can imagine. I like to think of a slight smile coming over his lips as he heard what his Master said.

"So that's it. That is what the kingdom will be. That is what the King will do."

For now he understood. It wasn't that Jesus was silent; it was that John had been listening for the wrong answer. John had been listening for an answer to his earthly problems, while Jesus was busy resolving his heavenly ones.

That's worth remembering the next time you hear the silence of God.

If you've asked for a mate, but are still sleeping alone . . . if you've asked for a child, but your womb stays barren . . . if you've asked for healing, but are still hurting . . . don't think God isn't listening. He is. And he is answering requests you are not even making.

Saint Teresa of Avila was insightful enough to pray, "Do not punish me by granting that which I wish or ask."[10]

The apostle Paul was honest enough to write, "We do not know what we ought to pray for."[11]

The fact is, John wasn't asking too much; he was asking too little. He was asking the Father to resolve the temporary, while Jesus was busy resolving the eternal. John was asking for immediate favor, while Jesus was orchestrating the eternal solution.

Does that mean that Jesus has no regard for injustice? No. He cares about persecutions. He cares about inequities and hunger and prejudice. And he knows what it is like to be punished for something he didn't do. He knows the meaning of the phrase, "It's just not right."

For it wasn't right that people spat into the eyes that had wept for them. It wasn't right that soldiers ripped chunks of flesh out of the back of their God. It wasn't right that spikes pierced the hands that formed the earth. And it wasn't right that the Son of God was forced to hear the silence of God.

It wasn't right, but it happened.

For while Jesus was on the cross, God *did* sit on his hands. He did turn his back. He did ignore the screams of the innocent.

He sat in silence while the sins of the world were placed upon his Son. And he did nothing while a cry a million times bloodier than John's echoed in the black sky: "My God, my God, why have you forsaken me?"[12]

Was it right? No.

Was it fair? No.

Was it love? Yes.

In a world of injustice, God once and for all tipped the scales in the favor of hope. And he did it by sitting on his hands so that we could know the kingdom of God.

CHAPTER EIGHTEEN

THE APPLAUSE
OF HEAVEN

Rejoice and be glad, because great is your reward. . . .

I'M ALMOST HOME. AFTER FIVE DAYS, FOUR HOTEL BEDS, ELEVEN restaurants, and twenty-two cups of coffee, I'm almost home. After eight airplane seats, five airports, two delays, one book, and five hundred thirteen packages of peanuts, I'm almost home.

The plane resonates under me. A baby cries behind me. Businessmen converse around me. Cool air blows from a hole above me. But all that matters is what is before me—home.

Home. It was my first thought when I awoke this morning. It was my first thought when I stepped down from the last podium.

It was my first thought when I said good-bye to my last host at the last airport.

There's no door like the one to your own house. There's no better place to put your feet than under your own table. There's no coffee like coffee out of your own mug. There's no meal like the one at your own table. And there's no embrace like the one from your own family.

Home. The longest part of going home is the last part—the plane's taxiing to the terminal from the runway. I'm the fellow the flight attendant always has to tell to sit down. I'm the guy with one hand on my briefcase and the other on my seat belt. I have learned that there is a critical split second in which I can bolt down the aisle into the first-class section before the tributaries of people begin emptying into the main aisle.

I don't do that on every flight. Only when I'm going home.

There is a leap of the heart as I exit the plane. I almost get nervous as I walk up the ramp. I step past people. I grip my satchel. My stomach tightens. My palms sweat. I walk into the lobby like an actor walking onto a stage. The curtain is lifted, and the audience stands in a half-moon. Most of the people see that I'm not the one they want and look past me.

But from the side I hear the familiar shriek of two little girls. "Daddy!" I turn and see them—faces scrubbed, standing on chairs, bouncing up and down in joy as the man in their life walks toward them. Jenna stops bouncing just long enough to clap. She applauds! I don't know who told her to do that, but you can bet I'm not going to tell her to stop.

Behind them I see a third face—little Sara, only a few months old. Deeply asleep, she furrows her brow slightly in reaction to the squealing.

And then I see a fourth face—my wife's face. Somehow, she has found time to comb her hair, put on a new dress, put on that extra sparkle. Somehow, though wrung out and done in, she will make me feel that my week is the only week worth talking about.

Faces of home.

That is what makes the promise at the end of the Beatitudes so compelling: "Rejoice and be glad, because great is your reward in heaven."

What is our reward? Home.

❧

The Book of Revelation could be entitled the Book of Homecoming, for in it we are given a picture of our heavenly home.

John's descriptions of the future steal your breath. His depiction of the final battle is graphic. Good clashes with evil. The sacred encounters the sinful. The pages howl with the shrieks of dragons and smolder with the coals of fiery pits. But in the midst of the battlefield there is a rose. John describes it in chapter 21:

> Then I saw a new heaven and a new earth, for the first heaven
> and the first earth had passed away, and there was no longer any
> sea. I saw the Holy City, the new Jerusalem, coming down out
> of heaven from God, prepared as a bride beautifully dressed for
> her husband. And I heard a loud voice from the throne saying,
> "Now the dwelling of God is with men, and he will live with
> them. They will be his people, and God himself will be with
> them and be their God. He will wipe every tear from their eyes.
> There will be no more death or mourning or crying or pain, for

the old order of things has passed away. He who was seated on the throne said, "I am making everything new!"[1]

John is old when he writes these words. His body is weary. The journey has taken its toll. His friends are gone. Peter is dead. Paul has been martyred. Andrew, James, Nathaniel . . . they are fuzzy figures from an early era.

As he hears the voice from the throne, I wonder, does he remember the day he heard it on the mountain? For it is the same John and the same Jesus. The same feet that followed Jesus up the mount so long ago now stand to follow him again. The same eyes that watched the Nazarene teach on the summit watch for him again. The same ears that heard Jesus first describe sacred delight listen to it revealed again.

In this final mountaintop encounter, God pulls back the curtain and allows the warrior to peek into the homeland. When given the task of writing down what he sees, John chooses the most beautiful comparison earth has to offer. The Holy City, John says, is like "a bride beautifully dressed for her husband."

What is more beautiful than a bride? One of the side benefits of being a minister is that I get an early glimpse of the bride as she stands at the top of the aisle. And I have to say that I have never seen an ugly bride. I've seen some grooms that could use an alteration or two, but never a bride. Maybe it is the aura of whiteness that clings to her as dew clings to a rose. Or perhaps it is the diamonds that glisten in her eyes. Or maybe it's the blush of love that pinks her cheeks or the bouquet of promises she carries. Whatever it is, there is the feeling that when you see a bride you are seeing the purest beauty the world can boast.

A bride. A commitment robed in elegance. "I'll be with you forever." Tomorrow bringing hope to today. Promised purity faithfully delivered.

When you read that our heavenly home is similar to a bride, tell me, doesn't it make you want to go home?

The world I woke up to this morning couldn't be described as a bride beautifully dressed for her husband, could yours?

Part of the world to which I awoke was grieving. A teenager took his life in the predawn darkness. No note. No explanation. Just a dumbstruck mother and a bewildered father who will forever be hounded by questions they cannot answer.

Part of the world to which I awoke was disillusioned. Another national leader has been accused of dishonesty. He blinked back tears and swallowed anger on network news. A generation ago, we would have given him the benefit of the doubt. Not now.

A part of the world to which I awoke this morning was devastated. A three-year-old's throat was cut open by her own father. A pre-med student was butchered and sacrificed by Satan worshipers. A husband of thirty years ran off with another man. (No, not a woman, a man.)

When you look at this world, stained by innocent blood and smudged with selfishness, doesn't it make you want to go home?

Me, too.

The old saint tells us that when we get home, God himself will wipe away our tears.

When I was a young man, I had plenty of people to wipe away my tears. I had two big sisters who put me under their wings. I had a dozen or so aunts and uncles. I had a mother who worked nights as a nurse and days as a mother—exercising both professions with tenderness. I even had a brother three years my elder who felt sorry for me occasionally.

But when I think about someone wiping away my tears, I think about Dad. His hands were callused and tough, his fingers short and stubby. And when my father wiped away a tear, he seemed to wipe it away forever. There was something in his touch that took away more than the drop of hurt from my cheek. It also took away my fear.

John says that someday God will wipe away your tears. The same hands that stretched the heavens will touch your cheeks. The same hands that formed the mountains will caress your face. The same hands that curled in agony as the Roman spike cut through will someday cup your face and brush away your tears. Forever.

When you think of a world where there will be no reason to cry, ever, doesn't it make you want to go home?

"There will be no more death . . ." John declares. Can you imagine it? A world with no hearses or morgues or cemeteries or tombstones? Can you imagine a world with no spades of dirt thrown on caskets? No names chiseled into marble? No funerals? No black dresses? No black wreaths?

If one of the joys of the ministry is a bride descending the church aisle, one of the griefs is a body encased in a shiny box in front of the pulpit. It's never easy to say good-bye. It's never easy to walk away. The hardest task in this world is to place a final kiss on cold lips that cannot kiss in return. The hardest thing in this world is to say good-bye.

In the next world, John says, "good-bye" will never be spoken. Tell me, doesn't that make you want to go home?

The most hopeful words of that passage from Revelation are those of God's resolve: "I am making everything new."

It's hard to see things grow old. The town in which I grew up is growing old. I was there recently. Some of the buildings are boarded up. Some of the houses are torn down. Some of my teachers are retired; some are buried. The old movie house where I took my dates has "For Sale" on the marquee, long since outdated by the newer theaters that give you eight choices. The only visitors to the drive-in theater are tumbleweeds and rodents. Memories of first dates and senior proms are weatherworn by the endless rain of years. High school sweethearts are divorced. A cheerleader died of an aneurysm. Our fastest halfback is buried only a few plots from my own father.

I wish I could make it all new again. I wish I could blow the dust off the streets. I wish I could walk through the familiar neighborhood, and wave at the familiar faces, and pet the familiar dogs, and hit one more home run in the Little League park. I wish I could walk down Main Street and call out the merchants that have retired and open the doors that have been boarded up. I wish I could make everything new . . . but I can't.

My mother still lives in the same house. You couldn't pay her to move. The house that seemed so big when I was a boy now feels tiny. On the wall are pictures of Mom in her youth—her hair autumn-brown, her face irresistibly beautiful. I see her now—still healthy, still vivacious, but with wrinkles, graying hair, slower step. Would that I could wave the wand and make everything new again. Would that I could put her once again in the strong embrace of the high-plains cowboy she loved and buried. Would that I could stretch out the wrinkles and take off the bifocals and restore the spring to her step. Would that I could make everything new . . . but I can't.

I can't. But God can. "He restores my soul,"[2] wrote the shepherd. He doesn't reform; he restores. He doesn't camouflage the old; he restores the new. The Master Builder will pull out the original plan and restore it. He will restore the vigor. He will restore the energy. He will restore the hope. He will restore the soul.

When you see how this world grows stooped and weary and then read of a home where everything is made new, tell me, doesn't that make you want to go home?

What would you give in exchange for a home like that? Would you really rather have a few possessions on earth than eternal possessions in heaven? Would you really choose a life of slavery to passion over a life of freedom? Would you honestly give up all of your heavenly mansions for a second-rate sleazy motel on earth?

"Great," Jesus said, "is your reward in heaven." He must have smiled when he said that line. His eyes must have danced, and his hand must have pointed skyward.

For he should know. It was his idea. It was his home.

⁓

I'll be home soon. My plane is nearing San Antonio. I can feel the nose of the jet dipping downward. I can see the flight attendants getting ready. Denalyn is somewhere in the parking lot, parking the car and hustling the girls toward the terminal.

I'll be home soon. The plane will land. I'll walk down that ramp and hear my name and see their faces. I'll be home soon.

You'll be home soon, too. You may not have noticed it, but you are closer to home than ever before. Each moment is a step taken. Each breath is a page turned. Each day is a mile marked, a mountain climbed. You are closer to home than you've ever been.

Before you know it, your appointed arrival time will come; you'll descend the ramp and enter the City.

You'll see faces that are waiting for you. You'll hear your name spoken by those who love you. And, maybe, just maybe—in the back, behind the crowds—the One who would rather die than live without you will remove his pierced hands from his heavenly robe and . . . applaud.

NOTES

CHAPTER 1 SACRED DELIGHT

1. 1 Timothy 1:11.
2. 1 Timothy 6:15.

CHAPTER 2 HIS SUMMIT

1. "How Americans Are Running Out of Time," *Time*, 24 April 1989, 74–76.
2. Matthew 11:28.
3. Walter Burkhardt, *Tell the Next Generation* (Ramsey, NJ: Paulist, 1982), 80, quoted in Brennan Manning, *Lion and Lamb* (Old Tappan, NJ: Chosen, Revell, 1986), 129.

CHAPTER 3 THE AFFLUENT POOR

1. His story is told in Matthew 19, Mark 10, and Luke 18.
2. Luke 18:27.

3. Mark 10:23.
4. Matthew 7:22.
5. Matthew 7:23.
6. Romans 8:3.
7. Frederick Dale Bruner clarifies this as he interprets Matthew 5:3: "Blessed are those who feel their poverty . . . and so cry out to heaven." *The Christbook: Matthew 1–12* (Waco, TX: Word, 1987), 135.
8. The word Jesus used for "poor" is a word which, when used in its most basic sense, "would not indicate the pauper, one so poor that he must daily work for his living, but the beggar, one who is dependent upon others for support." William Hendricksen, *Exposition of the Gospel of Matthew* (Grand Rapids, MI: Baker, 1973), 269.

CHAPTER 4 THE KINGDOM OF THE ABSURD

1. See Genesis 16–18, 21.
2. See Luke 5.
3. 2 Corinthians 12:9, TLB.
4. Philippians 3:4–6, TLB.
5. 1 Timothy 1:15.
6. Acts 22:16.
7. 1 Corinthians 1:23.
8. 1 Corinthians 1:23; Ephesians 2:8.
9. 2 Corinthians 5:14, NEB.

CHAPTER 5 THE PRISON OF PRIDE

1. 1 John 1:9, emphasis mine.
2. Bruner states it admirably: "God helps those who cannot help themselves and he helps those who try to help others, but he does not in any beatitude help those who think they can help

themselves—an often ungodly and antisocial conception." *The Christbook*, 152.

3. Matthew 14:28.

CHAPTER 6 TOUCHES OF TENDERNESS

1. Matthew 6:28–33.
2. Matthew 7:11.

CHAPTER 7 THE GLORY IN THE ORDINARY

1. See Exodus 4:1–4.
2. See 1 Samuel 17.
3. See John 9:1–6.

CHAPTER 8 THE BANDIT OF JOY

1. Ian Grey, *Stalin* (Garden City, NY: Doubleday, 1979), 457, and Alex De Jonge, *Stalin and the Shaping of the Soviet Union* (New York: William Morrow, 1986), 450.
2. "The Secret Life of Howard Hughes," *Time*, 13 December 1976, 22–41.
3. "John Lennon: In the Hard Day's Light," *People Weekly*, 15 August 1989, 68–69.
4. "In Praise of Courage," *Quest*, November 1980, 23.
5. See Matthew 10:1–28.
6. Matthew 10:21–22.
7. Matthew 10:26–31.
8. Matthew 10:26.
9. Hebrews 4:13; Daniel 2:22; Matthew 12:36; Psalm 90:8; 1 Corinthians 4:5.
10. Romans 8:1; 3:26; Acts 13:39; Hebrews 8:12; Colossians 3:3.
11. Hebrews 10:19; 22, emphasis mine.
12. Matthew 10:27–28.

13. Paul Harvey, *Paul Harvey's The Rest of the Story* (New York, NY: Bantam, 1977), 117.

CHAPTER 9 A SATISFIED THIRST

1. Luke 22:20.
2. Hebrews 10:4.
3. John 7:37.
4. "It is not sufficient that we merely want righteousness unless we have a downright famine for it . . ."—St. Jerome, quoted in Bruner, *The Christbook*, 142.
5. Matthew 26:28, PHILLIPS.

CHAPTER 11 THE FATHER IN THE FACE OF THE ENEMY

1. Archibald Hart, *The Hidden Link Between Adrenaline and Stress* (Waco, TX: Word, 1986), 101, 142–45.
2. Matthew 18:21–35.
3. Matthew 18:34.
4. Romans 2:4.

CHAPTER 12 THE STATE OF THE HEART

1. Proverbs 4:23.
2. Matthew 15:18–19.
3. Luke 6:45.
4. Psalm 51:10.

CHAPTER 14 SEEDS OF PEACE

1. James 3:18, TLB.
2. Paul Harvey, *Paul Harvey's The Rest of the Story* (New York, NY: Bantam, 1977), 49.
3. Isaiah 53:2, TLB.

CHAPTER 15 THE GREASY POLE OF POWER

1. *USA Today*, 22 March 1988, 5D.
2. Henry Emerson Fosdick, quoted in *A Guide to Prayer for Ministers and Other Servants* (Nashville: The Upper Room, 1983), 263.
3. Genesis 3:5.
4. Gary Smith, "Ali and His Entourage," *Sports Illustrated*, 16 April 1988, 48–49.
5. Paul Lee Tan, ed., *Encyclopedia of 7700 Illustrations* (Rockville, MD: Assurance Publishers, 1979), 1213–14.

CHAPTER 16 THE DUNGEON OF DOUBT

1. Matthew 14:1–12.
2. Matthew 11:2–3.
3. Philip Yancey, *Disappointment with God* (Grand Rapids, MI: Zondervan, 1988), 158.

CHAPTER 17 THE KINGDOM WORTH DYING FOR

1. Matthew 11:4–5.
2. Matthew 11:3.
3. Isaiah 35:5; 61:1.
4. Psalm 139:13.
5. Ephesians 2:10.
6. George Sweeting and Donald Sweeting, "The Evangelist and the Agnostic," *Moody Monthly*, July/August 1989, 69.
7. Ibid., 67.
8. Ibid., 69.
9. Ephesians 2:8–9.
10. Quoted in *A Guide to Prayer for Ministers and Other Servants*, 345.

11. Romans 8:26.
12. Matthew 27:46.

CHAPTER 18 THE APPLAUSE OF HEAVEN

1. Revelation 21:1–5.
2. Psalm 23:3.

STUDY GUIDE

Meeting Christ on the Mountain

THIS BOOK IS NOT AN END IN ITSELF.

If it does its job, it will lead you toward your own encounter with Christ on the mountain. And the following guide is intended to help you make that connection between reading a book and meeting the Christ.

This, then, is not so much a study of a book but a study of Christ's message and a catalyst for helping the book bring his message into the core of your life. It does not proceed chapter by chapter, but beatitude by beatitude, using the insights of the chapters as springboards for your own study and meditation.

There are ten study "sessions" here. If you are meeting together in a group, you might try to work through one a week. (Note to group leaders: since some of the questions in the guide are very personal, "sharing" answers should always be optional.) If you are studying on your own, go at your own pace, taking the time to let each beatitude work its transforming way into your attitude and character.

To each encounter, I suggest you bring your Bible and a notebook for writing down your own thoughts and observations. More important, bring a prayerful spirit and an expectant attitude. And when you come, plan to be surprised with the sacred delight of meeting Christ on the mountain.

≈

Session 1 Chapters 1 & 2

*Now when he saw the crowds, he went up on
a mountainside and sat down. . . . and he
began to teach them, saying: Blessed . . .*

1. Describe the happiest moment you can remember. Jot down some of the circumstances surrounding it—who was involved, when it happened, how long your happiness lasted. Now, recall the time in your life that you were most miserable. What was happening then? How have the circumstances of your life contributed to your happiness or unhappiness?

2. What is the difference between "choosing to be cheerful," as Beverly Sills describes it, and putting on a cheerful facade to cover up or deny misery? Under what circumstances, if any, could "choosing to be cheerful" be a negative choice?

3. The following Old Testament passages reveal some of the ideas about happiness Jesus' listeners had grown up on. How does each passage describe a happy (blessed) person?

- Psalm 1:1–6
- Psalm 2:10–12
- Psalm 32:1–2; 5–7; 10–11
- Psalm 41:1–3
- Psalm 84:4–5; 11–12
- Psalm 94:12–13
- Psalm 112:1–9
- Proverbs 8:1–2; 32–36 (note who is "speaking")

4. Chapter 1 states that the Greek word Jesus used for "blessed" in the Beatitudes (*makarios*) is the same one used by Paul to describe God. It was used in other ancient literature to describe the "happy state of the gods above earthly sufferings" and to denote "a transcendent happiness of a life beyond care, labor and death" (*Theological Dictionary of the New Testament*, 4:362). What does Jesus' use of this powerful word say about the kind of happiness he is promising?

5. Read Matthew 4:23–25. What events in Jesus' ministry immediately preceded Jesus' withdrawing to the mountain? What do you think was the significance of this order of events? Why did Jesus withdraw to the mountain with his disciples at this particular time?

6. What are the best times and places for you to "go to the mountain"? What specific activities and responsibilities tend to stand in the way of your getting there?

---

7. Chapter 1 states that "you are one decision away from joy." Chapter 2 says that "the mountain is only a decision away." Specifically, what decision is this?

Session 2 Chapters 3 & 4

Blessed are the poor in spirit, for theirs is the kingdom of heaven.

1. How does chapter 3 interpret being "poor in spirit"? How does this compare with any previous ideas you had about what this beatitude means?

2. Luke's version of this beatitude (found in Luke 6:20, 24) omits the "in spirit" idea entirely; it simply states that "the rich" have their reward here and therefore cannot expect a reward in heaven. And Jesus tells the rich young ruler directly that "it is hard for a rich man to enter the kingdom of heaven" (Matthew 19:23–24). Do you think the first beatitude applies especially to those who are poor in material possessions? If not, why does Matthew make these specific comments about material wealth? (You may find some ideas in the endnotes for this chapter.)

3. List three reasons why being poor in spirit as described in these two chapters is difficult for most of us. Why do we have such a hard time admitting our own inadequacy and failures even to God and ourselves?

4. List what you consider your five greatest strengths and your five greatest weaknesses. Then examine your list in light of chapter 3. Does being poor in spirit mean denying your

strengths or not trying to improve your weaknesses? Does it mean being "down on yourself"? Why or why not?

5. Is it possible to be both arrogant and insecure at the same time? What do you think are the motives behind the rich young ruler's self-justification and overachievement?

6. What is the difference between trying to achieve salvation and trying to please God? Between being poor in spirit and being a poor steward of your God-given gifts?

7. Read the following parables describing the "kingdom of heaven": Matthew 13:24–33, 44–50. What additional insight do these parables give about the nature of the "kingdom" in which the poor in spirit will live?

8. Read Matthew 16:13–20, which tells the circumstances under which Peter's name was changed and he was given the "keys to the kingdom of heaven." What elements of this account point to Peter's being poor in spirit? What does this passage tell you about the nature of the kingdom?

9. What sort of positive change would you like in your life? According to these two chapters, what would be your best strategy for such change?

SESSION 3 CHAPTERS 5 & 6

Blessed are those who mourn, for they will be comforted.

1. After reading these two chapters, complete the sentence: "Blessed are those who mourn, for . . ." What specific kind of grief do these chapters speak of?

2. Can you think of cases in which admitting failure can become a cop-out—an excuse to stop trying? What (if any) is the difference between "mourning" and giving in to failure?

3. Most of our everyday situations aren't as dramatic as that of Anibal or Peter; the life-or-death nature of our decisions isn't as obvious. How can we be more aware of our need for Jesus in noncrisis situations?

4. Read Hosea 7:14 and 2 Corinthians 7:9–11. What kind of mourning do they describe? Is it included under Jesus' blessing in the second beatitude?

5. To what things, people, or activities (adult versions of the hug, the Band-Aid, the flashlight) do you tend to turn for comfort? Do they work? In your opinion, is anything inherently wrong with such "security blankets"?

6. Practically speaking, what does God's comfort feel like? What form does it take, and how does it come to us? Have you ever felt it? (For ideas, see Genesis 5:29; 24:67; 1 Chronicles 7:22; Job 6:10; Psalms 23:4; 71:21; 77; 119:50–52; 40:1–5; Isaiah 52:7–9; 57:14–19; John 11:19; 14:1–6; 15:15–22; 2 Corinthians 1:3–4; 7:6–7.)

7. Why do you think so many of us come to think that God doesn't want to hear about our problems or gets tired of forgiving us?

8. Read 2 Corinthians 1:3–4. Under what circumstances are we called upon to be agents of God's comfort to those who mourn?

9. List three ways we can comfort others effectively. What are some tactics that do *not* work? Describe a situation in which you were able to provide comfort.

10. What is the relationship between "mourning" and being poor in spirit? How are the two alike? How are they different?

SESSION 4 CHAPTERS 7 & 8

Blessed are the meek, for they will inherit the earth.

1. How does chapter 7 interpret the word *meek*? How does that definition differ from your previous ideas of "meekness?"

2. Do you think of yourself as "ordinary"? Why or why not? Do you find that description comforting or insulting?

3. What are some synonyms for the word *meek* as it is used in the Beatitudes? For ideas, look up Numbers 12:3; Psalm 25:9; Isaiah 11:4; 61:1; Matthew 11:29; and 1 Peter 3:4 in the King James Version and another translation.

4. Practically speaking, what does it mean to be meek in the sense of letting God use you? If he doesn't speak through an angel or a burning bush, how do you know what he wants you to do?

5. In practical terms, how do you avoid taking over or "telling God how to do his job"—and still get something done?

6. Chapter 6 interprets "inherit the earth" as not being intimidated or afraid of any earthly power or person. In your mind, is this a satisfactory definition? Would you be more comfortable saying, "Blessed are the meek, for theirs is the kingdom of heaven"? Why do you think Jesus specified "the earth" in this beatitude?

7. Psalm 37:11 also states that the meek will inherit the earth. Read Psalm 37:1–17 to understand this verse in context. What is the message of the psalm? Is its thrust basically similar to or different from the third beatitude? What new perspective does Psalm 37 give to Jesus' statement?

---

8. Describe one time in your life when you let fear keep you from doing something you knew you should do.

9. According to chapter 8, what are the three ways we seek to handle our fears? To which of these three are you more likely to turn? (Don't be misled by the 'big guy' examples; these defense mechanisms take many forms—major and minor!). Give an example of a time when you have taken refuge in one of these defenses.

10. What reason did Jesus give the disciples for not being afraid? Why can this be taken as a source of courage?

11. What would you do tomorrow if you were guaranteed you couldn't fail and that nothing could hurt you? Write down and/or share one example.

SESSION 5 CHAPTERS 9 & 10

*Blessed are those who hunger and thirst for
righteousness, for they will be filled.*

1. A "how to write fiction" computer software program currently on the market begins its instruction with a question: "What does _____ want?" The idea is that all plots (and therefore, all stories) arise from people's basic needs and desires. If you were writing a novel about yourself, how would you answer that starting question? What "hungers and thirsts" motivate you most?

2. How does chapter 9 interpret the idea of righteousness? What would your own definition be?

3 Read Matthew 23:27–28. What was there about the Pharisees' attitude about righteousness that made Jesus so angry?

4. Read Romans 3:10–31. What do this passage and Matthew 23:27–28 tell us about trying to be righteous in our own right, boasting about our righteousness, or assuming we are righteous because we "keep all the rules"? How are these attitudes different from "hungering and thirsting" for righteousness?

5. According to chapters 9 and 10 and Romans 3:21–31, what is the only way our "hunger and thirst for righteousness" can be "satisfied"?

6. According to chapter 9, what is the ultimate reason that those who hunger and thirst after righteousness will be filled?

7. What does "hungering and thirsting after righteousness" have to do with "holding earthly possessions in open palms" and being dependent on Jesus for joy (chapter 10)?

8. Chapter 10 intimates that our fullest experience of "being filled" will be in heaven. But do we ever experience such satisfaction here on earth? If so, how?

9. Look back over the first three beatitudes. What do they have in common? How is this fourth beatitude like them? How is it different?

SESSION 6 CHAPTER 11

Blessed are the merciful, for they will be shown mercy.

1. According to chapter 11, what is the opposite of mercy?

2. Read Matthew 6:12 and 7:1–2. What light do these passages

from later in the Sermon on the Mount throw on the idea of the merciful receiving mercy?

3. Is mercy synonymous with forgiveness? Why or why not?

4. Why is it so hard to give up resentments? What does mercy cost us?

5. In what ways does resentment harm us? List three specific negative effects.

6. According to chapter 12, what makes it possible for us to be merciful and forgiving?

7. Write one to five things to do in the next week either to make restitution for hurts you have caused or to reach out in forgiveness to those who have hurt you. (Be honest with yourself. If you cannot bring yourself yet to forgive those who have hurt you or to accept God's forgiveness for hurts you have caused, simply write down that you will pray for the ability to do these things.)

SESSION 7 CHAPTERS 12 & 13

Blessed are the pure in heart, for they will see God.

1. Does the fact that "what comes out of us" makes us good or evil mean that what goes in doesn't matter much? Why or why not?

2. Look up 1 Kings 18:26–28 and Acts 22:3. Is purity the same as sincerity or good intentions? Can a person be both pure and wrong?

3. Look up 1 Peter 1:22; 1 Timothy 1:5–8; and John 8:31–32. What principles determine purity of heart?

4. Now back up and read Matthew 22:34–40. What, according to this passage, is the key to achieving purity of heart?

5. Must we always wait until our "insides are clean" before we start to act right—and before we see God? Why or why not?

6. Look up John 14:5–14. What does John have to say about how we come to "see God"? What different perspective does that give to the idea of being pure in heart?

7. According to chapter 13, what is the difference between "temple builders" and "Savior seekers"?

8. Give an example of a time you, or someone you know, got so caught up in a project you forgot the whole point of it. Have you ever been so involved in church or religious activities that you got out of touch with God?

9. At what time in your life have you been most aware of "seeing God"? At what times have you been able to "see" him only in retrospect? What is the difference between "temple building" and the "dry times" every Christian experiences?

10. If "Savior seekers" often must find Jesus "in spite of" the temple, what is the purpose of the organized church? What can we do better in community that we cannot do as individual seekers?

SESSION 8 CHAPTERS 14 & 15

Blessed are the peacemakers, for they will be called sons of God.

1. How would you define peace as it is portrayed in chapter 14? How does this concept of peace differ from more common ideas about peace?

---

2. Commentator Dale Bruner writes, "We can almost translate the key word here, 'peacemakers,' with the word 'whole-makers.' . . . Biblical *shalom* conveys the picture of a circle; it means comprehensive well-being in every direction and relation. . . . If we could translate 'blessed are the circle makers' and make sense, we would. To make peace, in Scripture, is to bring community. 'Peacemakers are reconcilers'" (*The Christbook*, 149). How do the examples of peacemaking given in this chapter fit Bruner's definition?

3. Read at least three of the following Scriptures: Numbers 6:24–26; Psalm 29:11; Luke 1:76–79; John 14:27; 16:33; Romans 5:1; 1 Corinthians 14:33; Galatians 5:22; Ephesians 2:14–17; and Philippians 4:7. According to these passages and to chapter 14, what is the ultimate source of peace?

4. Read James 3:13–18. What are some of the "prerequisites" for peacemaking? What must happen inside us before we can be peacemakers?

5. Read Matthew 10:34–39. Are there times when peacemaking in the larger sense involves accepting conflict rather than avoiding it? Does it ever involve *initiating* conflict? If possible, give a biblical or contemporary example.

6. Is it enough simply to plant seeds of peace? Are there ways we can nurture them and help them grow?

7. Is the "push for power" a basic part of human nature? Can it ever be a positive thing? How can we avoid it?

8. How does power relate to peacemaking? Can power ever be used in the *service* of peacemaking? Why or why not?

9. Write down the names of three people in your life who could use a word or act of peace from you. Beside each person's

name, write an idea for a "seed" of peace. Finally, write down a specific date and time to plant your seed and commit to that schedule. If you are meeting in a group, be prepared to share your "peace seed" (not necessarily the results) at the next meeting. If you are on your own, consider sharing your peace initiatives with a friend and asking to be held accountable.

Session 9 Chapters 16 & 17

Blessed are those who are persecuted because of righteousness, for theirs is the kingdom of God.

1. According to chapter 16, why did John send word to ask Jesus if he was really the Messiah?
2. Name a situation in which you have felt persecuted for doing what was right. What was the outcome of your experience?
3. What are some of the explanations you've heard for times when God seems silent? Which explanations seemed most satisfactory? Which didn't satisfy you?
4. Do persecution and "God's silence" always go hand in hand, or are they two separate things? Why do you think so?
5. What are some ways (subtle and overt) that Christians are persecuted "because of righteousness"?
6. Read Proverbs 21:2 and Jeremiah 17:9. What do these passages suggest about how we can interpret the bad things that happen to us? If we are in trouble, how can we be sure that our persecution is "because of righteousness"—that we are in trouble for the right reasons?

7. Chapter 17 states, "God has never turned away the questions of a sincere searcher." Do you feel comfortable with this idea of questioning God? Why or why not? When you get to heaven, what are some questions you want to ask him?

8. The Book of Job is another biblical account of a person who suffered from God's seeming silence in the face of injustice. When struck with numerous, undeserved afflictions, he, too, questioned God. But Job's questions were different, as were the answers he received and the outcome of the story.

- Read Job 3:23; 7:20–21; 10:2–7; 13:20–24; 24:1–12. What questions did Job ask God?

- Read Job 38:1–21; 40:1–14; and 42:1–6. What was God's answer? How was it similar to Jesus' answer to John? How was it different?

9. Write down the three characteristics of Christ's kingdom that are implied in Jesus' answer to John. In what ways have you seen these characteristics continuing in your lifetime?

10. Chapter 17 relates this beatitude back to the first one, "Blessed are the poor in spirit," which also states "for theirs is the kingdom of heaven." Why do you think the phrase was repeated? How does being poor in spirit relate to being persecuted for the sake of righteousness?

11. Read Jesus' familiar model prayer cited in Matthew 6:9–13. In your opinion, how do Jesus' instructions on how to pray relate to the way we respond to persecution and doubt?

Session 10 Chapter 18

Rejoice and be glad, because great is your reward. . . .

1. According to chapter 18, what is the ultimate joy promised to those who follow Jesus?
2. Describe the happiest homecoming you have ever experienced. Who was there? Why were you (or someone else) coming home? Where had you (or the homecomer) been? Why was this particular experience so happy?
3. According to chapter 18, what biblical images does the Book of Revelation use to describe our "homeland"? What do these biblical pictures say about our future with Christ?
4. What kinds of experiences (personal or secondhand) in this world make you "want to go home" to a world made new? How do you picture your heavenly home?
5. What do the Beatitudes tell us about how we receive "the applause of heaven" while still on earth?
6. Read Luke's version of the Beatitudes as given in Luke 6:20–26. How do the two versions differ? Where do they agree? What different perspective does Luke's account give to Jesus' picture of sacred delight?
7. Most of us tend to think of the beatitudes as cause-and-effect statements: If you become poor in spirit, then—as a result—you will see God. If you mourn your sins, then you will be comforted. They therefore tend to be thought of as requirements—"rules to live by" that are almost impossible to live up to. For a different perspective, conclude this study by turning the "cause and effect" idea around a bit. Think

of all the beatitudes as effects—descriptions of what happens when we accept Christ. If you look at each beatitude this way, the two parts of each beatitude can be seen as two stages or dimensions: the immediate, earthly effect and the ultimate or spiritual effect. With this idea in mind, fill in the chart for each beatitude, using the chapters of this book for a resource. The first is filled in below to give an example.

BEATITUDE	CAUSE	RESULT	ULTIMATE RESULT
Blessed are the poor in spirit, for theirs is the kingdom of God.	We truly respond to the reality of who Christ is and who we are . . .	. . . we become acutely aware of where we fall short; we become poor in spirit.	. . . we become citizens of Christ's heavenly kingdom; we receive a new name and identity.
Blessed are those who mourn, for they will be comforted.	We truly respond to the reality of who Christ is and who we are . . .		
Blessed are the meek, for they shall inherit the earth.	We truly respond to the reality of who Christ is and who we are . . .		
Blessed are those who hunger and thirst for righteousness, for they will be comforted.	We truly respond to the reality of who Christ is and who we are . . .		

BEATITUDE	CAUSE	RESULT	ULTIMATE RESULT
Blessed are the merciful, for they will be shown mercy.	We truly respond to the reality of who Christ is and who we are . . .		
Blessed are the pure in heart, for they will see God.	We truly respond to the reality of who Christ is and who we are . . .		
Blessed are the peacemakers, for they will be called sons of God.	We truly respond to the reality of who Christ is and who we are . . .		
Blessed are those who are persecuted because of righteousness, for theirs is the kingdom of heaven.	We truly respond to the reality of who Christ is and who we are . . .		

The Lucado Reader's Guide

Discover . . . Inside every book by Max Lucado, you'll find words of
encouragement and inspiration that will draw you into a deeper experience with
Jesus and treasures for your walk with God. What will you discover?

3:16: The Numbers of Hope
... the 26 words that can change
your life.
core scripture: John 3:16

And the Angels Were Silent
... what Jesus Christ's final days can
teach you about what matters most.
core scripture: Matthew 20–27

The Applause of Heaven
... the secret to a truly satisfying life.
core scripture: The Beatitudes,
Matthew 5:1–10

Come Thirsty
... how to rehydrate your heart
and sink into the wellspring of
God's love.
core scripture: John 7:37–38

Cure for the Common Life
... the unique things God designed
you to do with your life.
core scripture: 1 Corinthians 12:7

Facing Your Giants
... when God is for you,
no challenge is too great.
core scripture: 1 and 2 Samuel

Fearless
... how faith is the antidote to
the fear in your life.
core scripture: John 14:1, 3

Grace
... the incredible gift that saves
and sustains you.
core scripture: Hebrews 12:15

A Gentle Thunder
... the God who will do whatever it
takes to lead his children back to him.
core scripture: Psalm 81:7

Great Day, Every Day
... how living in a purposeful way
will help you trust more, stress less.
core scripture: Psalm 118:24

The Great House of God
... a blueprint for peace, joy, and
love found in the Lord's Prayer.
core scripture: The Lord's Prayer,
Matthew 6:9–13

God Came Near
... a love so great that it left heaven
to become part of your world.
core scripture: John 1:14

He Chose the Nails
... a love so deep that it chose death
on a cross—just to win your heart.
core scripture: 1 Peter 1:18–20

He Still Moves Stones
... the God who still does the
impossible—in your life.
core scripture: Matthew 12:20

In the Eye of the Storm
... peace in the storms of your life.
core scripture: John 6

In the Grip of Grace
... the greatest gift of all—the
grace of God.
core scripture: Romans

It's Not About Me
... why focusing on God will make
sense of your life.
core scripture: 2 Corinthians 3:18

Just Like Jesus
... a life free from guilt, fear,
and anxiety.
core scripture: Ephesians 4:23–24

A Love Worth Giving
... how living loved frees you
to love others.
core scripture: 1 Corinthians 13

Next Door Savior
... a God who walked life's
hardest trials—and still walks
with you through yours.
core scripture: Matthew 16:13–16

**No Wonder They Call Him
the Savior**
... hope in the unlikeliest place—
upon the cross.
core scripture: Romans 5:15

Outlive Your Life
... that a great God created you
to do great things.
core scripture: Acts 1

Six Hours One Friday
... forgiveness and healing in
the middle of loss and failure.
core scripture: John 19–20

Traveling Light
... the power to release the burdens
you were never meant to carry.
core scripture: Psalm 23

**When God Whispers
Your Name**
... the path to hope in knowing that
God knows you, never forgets you, and
cares about the details of your life.
core scripture: John 10:3

When Christ Comes
... why the best is yet to come.
core scripture: 1 Corinthians 15:23

You'll Get Through This
... hope in the midst of your hard
times and a God who uses the mess
of life for good.
core scripture: Genesis 50:20

Recommended reading if you're struggling with . . .

FEAR AND WORRY
Come Thirsty
Fearless
For the Tough Times
Next Door Savior
Traveling Light

DISCOURAGEMENT
He Still Moves Stones
Next Door Savior

GRIEF/DEATH OF A LOVED ONE
Next Door Savior
Traveling Light
When Christ Comes
When God Whispers Your Name
You'll Get Through This

GUILT
In the Grip of Grace
Just Like Jesus

LONELINESS
God Came Near

SIN
Facing Your Giants
He Chose the Nails
Six Hours One Friday

WEARINESS
When God Whispers Your Name
You'll Get Through This

Recommended reading if you want to know more about . . .

THE CROSS
And the Angels Were Silent
He Chose the Nails
No Wonder They Call Him the Savior
Six Hours One Friday

GRACE
Grace
He Chose the Nails
In the Grip of Grace

HEAVEN
The Applause of Heaven
When Christ Comes

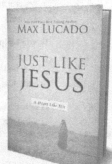

SHARING THE GOSPEL
God Came Near
Grace
No Wonder They Call Him the Savior

Recommended reading if you're looking for more . . .

COMFORT
For the Tough Times
He Chose the Nails
Next Door Savior
Traveling Light
You'll Get Through This

COMPASSION
Outlive Your Life

COURAGE
Facing Your Giants
Fearless

HOPE
3:16: The Numbers of Hope
Facing Your Giants
A Gentle Thunder
God Came Near
Grace

JOY
The Applause of Heaven
Cure for the Common Life
When God Whispers Your Name

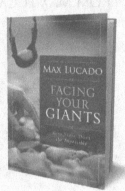

LOVE
Come Thirsty
A Love Worth Giving
No Wonder They Call Him the Savior

PEACE
And the Angels Were Silent
The Great House of God
In the Eye of the Storm
Traveling Light
You'll Get Through This

SATISFACTION
And the Angels Were Silent
Come Thirsty
Cure for the Common Life
Great Day Every Day

TRUST
A Gentle Thunder
It's Not About Me
Next Door Savior

Max Lucado books make great gifts!
If you're coming up to a special occasion, consider one of these.

FOR ADULTS:
For the Tough Times
Grace for the Moment
Live Loved
The Lucado Life Lessons Study Bible
Mocha with Max
DaySpring Daybrighteners® and cards

FOR TEENS/GRADUATES:
Let the Journey Begin
You Can Be Everything God Wants You to Be
You Were Made to Make a Difference

FOR KIDS:
Just in Case You Ever Wonder
The Oak Inside the Acorn
You Are Special

FOR PASTORS AND TEACHERS:
God Thinks You're Wonderful
You Changed My Life

AT CHRISTMAS:
The Crippled Lamb
Christmas Stories from Max Lucado
God Came Near

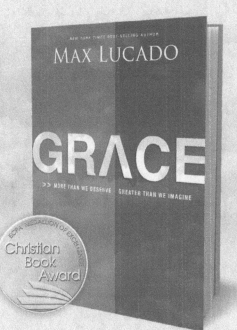